Easy Paper-Pieced

BABY QUILTS

CAROL DOAK

Martingale™
& COMPANY

Credits

President • Nancy J. Martin
CEO • Daniel J. Martin
Publisher • Jane Hamada
Editorial Director • Mary V. Green
Design and Production Manager • Stan Green
Editorial Project Manager • Tina Cook
Technical Editor • Ursula Reikes
Copy Editor • Del Lausa
Illustrator • Laurel Strand
Photographer • Brent Kane
Text and Cover Designer • Trina Stahl

That Patchwork Place® is an imprint of Martingale & Company.™

Easy Paper-Pieced Baby Quilts

Martingale & Company
20205 144th Avenue NE
Woodinville, WA 98072-8478 USA
www.patchwork.com

Printed in Hong Kong
06 05 04 03 02 01 8 7 6 5 4 3 2 1

Mission Statement

We are dedicated to providing quality products and service by working together to inspire creativity and to enrich the lives we touch.

JS JB

Library of Congress Cataloging-in-Publication Data

Doak, Carol.
Easy paper-pieced baby quilts / Carol Doak.
p. cm.
ISBN 1-56477-330-2
1. Patchwork—Patterns. 2. Appliqué—Patterns. 3. Children's quilts. I. Title.

TT835.D625 2001
746.46'041—dc21

00–065357

Dedication

To my granddaughter Jessie Ann Doak,

who will bring her baby quilt, made with love, into the next generation.

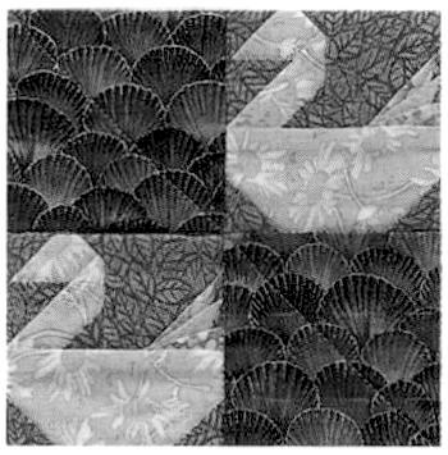

Acknowledgments

My heartfelt thanks and appreciation go to:

Ellen Peters for her beautiful machine quilting.

Alice M. Bachraty for sharing the thread-clipping tip.

Ursula Reikes for her friendship and editing expertise.

My friends and family for their love and support.

Everyone at Martingale & Company who took my manuscript and turned it into a beautiful book.

CONTENTS

PREFACE

OF COURSE, we were excited and thrilled when my son, Brian, and his wife, Lisa, announced that they were going to have a baby in the spring. As I looked forward to the arrival of my grandchild, I naturally considered several baby quilt ideas. Because I love designing and paper piecing, I simply couldn't resist designing paper-pieced baby quilts. It was great fun to consider baby themes for the block designs, then use bright and lively colors to bring them to life. But, making these small quilts offered instant gratification, and I had as much fun making them as I did designing them. Since I didn't know whether we would be blessed with a granddaughter or a grandson, I designed several quilts that would be appropriate for either, as well as a number of quilts specifically for a boy or a girl.

Now I am pleased and excited to share these quilt designs with you. Whether they are destined for a charity project, a friend's baby, your grandchild, or your own new baby, I hope you enjoy making these quick and easy paper-pieced baby quilts as much as I did.

INTRODUCTION

WHETHER YOU are an experienced quilter or a novice, paper piecing is an easy technique for creating accurate patchwork. This book will give you all the information you need to make a baby quilt from beginning to end. You'll learn how to get started, how to paper piece, and how to finish your baby quilt, step by step. The "Tools and Supplies" section contains a list of those items that will assist you in making your baby quilt. (When it comes to helpful quilt tools, my motto is "Life is too short to want"!)

In "Fabric," you will learn about fabric grain as it relates to paper foundation piecing and about the helpful cutting charts you will use to cut the fabric pieces for your baby quilt. "Paper Foundations" describes the process for making the foundations, and "Paper-Piecing Techniques" will walk you through the general steps for making paper-pieced units for the quilts. In "Quilt-Top Assembly" you'll learn how to assemble the units into a complete quilt top.

Directions for each of the quilts in "Baby Quilts" include a quilt layout, yardage requirements, quilt components, a fabric cutting chart, and helpful tips to ensure your success. Lastly, "Quilt Finishing" will guide you through the completion of your baby quilt for presentation to that special baby.

GETTING STARTED

TOOLS AND SUPPLIES

MANY YEARS ago, my husband shared with me his opinion that he needed to have the right tool to do a job correctly. I have taken those words to heart and applied them to my quiltmaking. It seems silly not to use any tool that will make what I do easier, and therefore much more enjoyable. The following items will make your paper-piecing experience both easy and fun.

6" Add-a-Quarter™ ruler: This tool is invaluable for trimming the fabric pieces so you know exactly where to place the next piece of fabric (see "Resources" on page 95).

Olfa rotary point cutter: Use this tool when you want to unsew a seam.

Open-toe presser foot: This foot will allow you to see the needle go into the lines on the paper foundation.

Papers for Foundation Piecing: Use this lightweight paper when you copy the foundation piecing designs (see "Resources" on page 95).

Postcard: Use a sturdy postcard or 3" x 5" card to fold the paper foundation back neatly on the next sewing line in order to trim the previously sewn fabric piece(s).

Rotary cutter and rotary mat: Choose a larger rotary cutter that will allow you to cut through several layers of fabric at once.

Rotary rulers: The 6" x 12" and the 6" x 6" rotary rulers are helpful for cutting the fabric and trimming the blocks.

Sandpaper tabs: Place stick-on sandpaper tabs every 3" along the length, and ½" in from the edge, of the rotary ruler. This will prevent the ruler from slipping on the paper when trimming.

Scotch brand removable tape: This tape will be helpful if you need to repair a foundation or resew across a previously sewn line.

Sewing thread: Use a standard 50-weight sewing thread. Match the thread to the general value of the fabrics. In most cases, you can rely upon white, medium gray, and black threads.

Silk pins with small heads: Because you will be pinning your first piece and then placing a postcard on top of the pin, use pins with small heads that won't get in your way.

Size 90/14 sewing machine needles: These large needles will perforate the paper nicely, making it easier to remove later.

Small stick-on notes: Label your stacks of cut fabric pieces with these. They'll keep you organized and save time.

Stapler and staple remover: Use a stapler to secure several foundations for trimming, and the remover to remove the staple after trimming.

Thread clippers: A pair of thread clippers with narrow blades is handy for clipping threads from both the top and the bottom of the foundation at the same time (see page 15 and "Resources" on page 95).

Tweezers: Use tweezers to remove small bits of paper left behind in the intersecting seams.

Fabric

For the pictorial baby quilts, I chose colorful fabrics that represent the themes of the picture, rather than typical baby print fabrics. For quilts that are not pictorial, I used a multicolored fabric as the "main player," which then served as the inspiration for grouping the remainder of the colors in the quilts. This main player fabric can be playful like the cat fabric in "Little Boy Love" (see page 52), or a colorful print like the border in "Pinwheels" (see page 40). If you select coordinating fabrics based on colors found within the main player fabric, you won't need to rely upon imagination to see how all your colors work together. You'll be able to see them all right there in the main player pattern.

You might coordinate your fabrics with a multicolored print like the leaf design shown here.

Fabric Grain

When selecting your fabrics for the block designs, it is helpful to understand the concepts of fabric grain as they relate to paper piecing. The good news is that you can ignore fabric grain for mechanical reasons because the paper foundation supports the fabric to prevent stretching. However, because you will be placing fabric pieces in different directions along the seam lines on the foundation, the fabric will open and lay in different directions. Choose a nondirectional print fabric for the background area to avoid the distraction of seeing the print going in several different directions. In the following example, the fabric selected for the background of the tree block is directional in the first block and nondirectional in the second block. This same premise is true if one element inside the block is composed of several pieces of the same fabric placed in different directions.

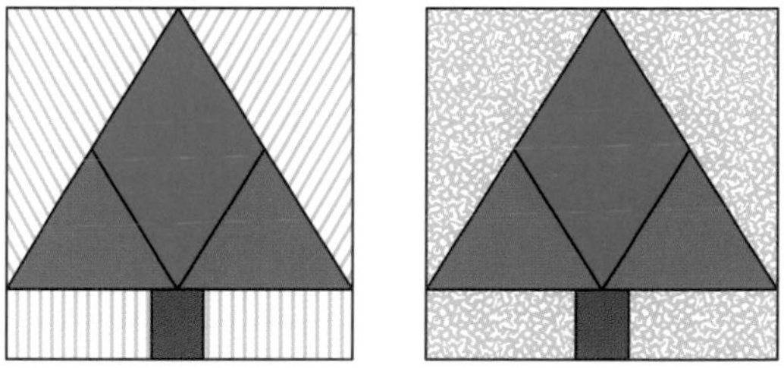

The following information about directional fabric will make your paper-piecing project go more smoothly and help you achieve the results you want.

Vertical and Horizontal Seams: If you place the straight grain edge of the fabric along a vertical or horizontal seam, the fabric will open to the straight grain. In the following example of the barn block, a directional red check is placed along the vertical and horizontal seams that complete the barn siding. You can see that the direction of the check is consistent.

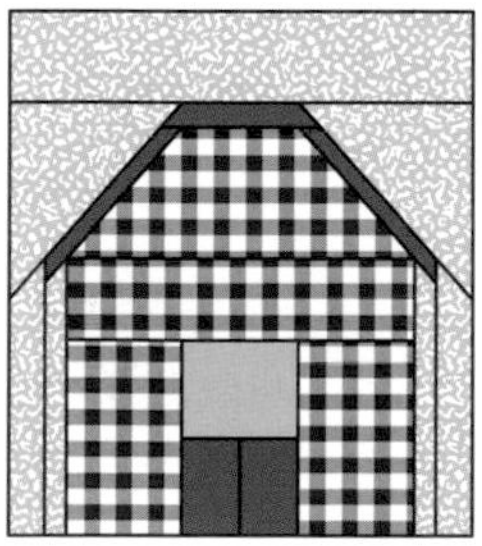

If a directional fabric is used more than once within the block, you need to consider how each piece will be placed when cutting your fabric pieces so that the direction will be consistent. In that instance, consider avoiding the use of directional fabrics so you will have less to consider when cutting your fabric pieces. Note the striped fabric used in the barn block illustration below. In the first case the stripes are consistent, and in the second they are not.

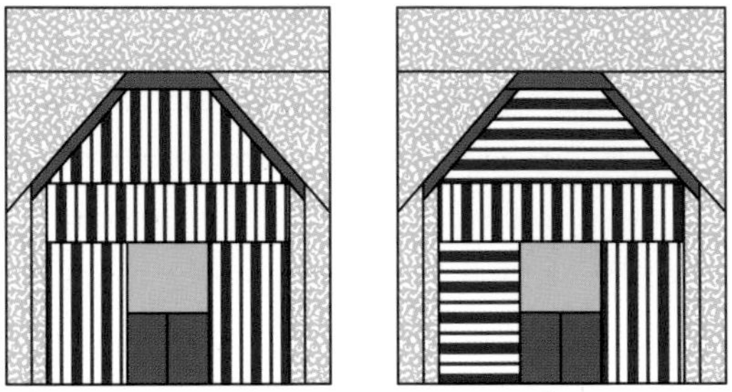

Directional fabric consistent

Directional fabric inconsistent

45° Seams: If you place a bias edge along a 45° seam, the fabric will open to the straight grain. In the following heart block, half-square triangles are used for the small and large corner triangles so that the fabric will open to the straight grain. A quarter-square triangle is used for the center triangle

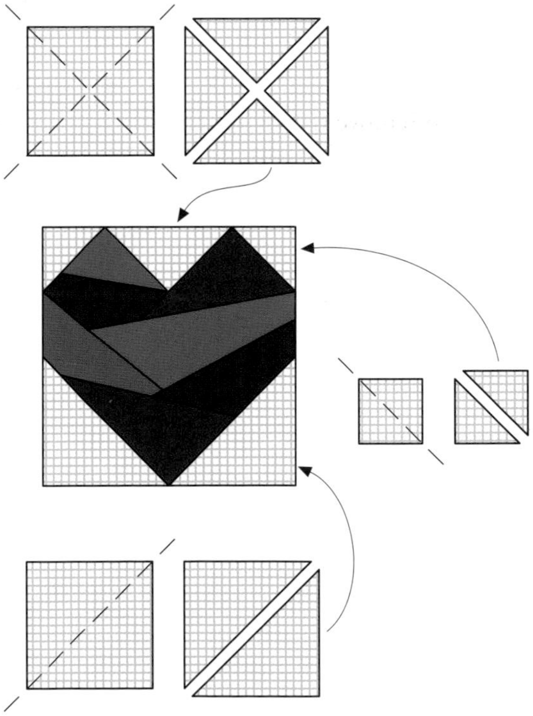

"Weird Angle Seams": I refer to all the other seams in a block as weird angle seams. It is possible to cut the fabric so it will open to the straight grain when placed along weird angle seams. However, in order to provide simple cutting lists for these baby quilts, I chose to cut the fabric pieces as strips where the fabric won't open to the straight of grain when placed along weird angle seams. For this reason, it is best to choose nondirectional fabric for these pieces.

I realize that the above information may be more than some readers want to know. The good news is that you don't have to worry about these issues if you simply follow my lead and use nondirectional fabrics where I used them in my baby quilts. Nondirectional fabrics are indicated in the materials lists. If there is no indication, you can use a directional fabric without complications.

Cutting Charts

A cutting chart is provided for each quilt project. Cut the binding, borders, and setting pieces across the width of the fabric first, then cut the pieces for the paper-pieced blocks. When you see the ⧅ symbol in the cutting chart, cut the square(s) once diagonally to make two half-square triangles.

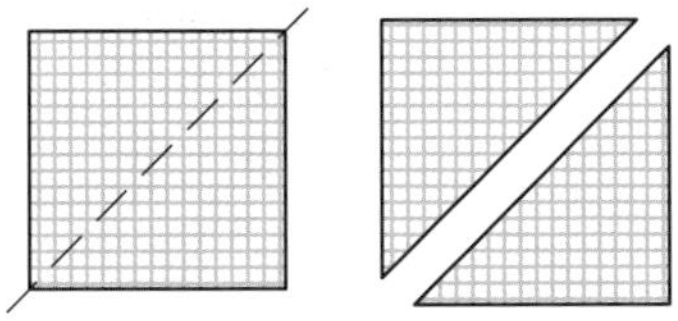

Square cut into half-square triangles

When you see the ⧅ symbol, cut the squares twice diagonally to make four quarter-square triangles.

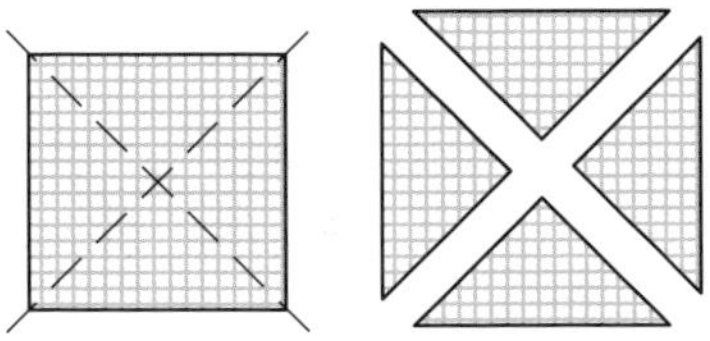

Square cut into quarter-square triangles

The easiest way to cut squares and rectangles is to start with a strip of fabric in the required width. Cut pieces from a single layer if you only need a few pieces. Fold the strip in half or quarters and cut pieces from multiple layers if you need several pieces from the same fabric.

As you cut the pieces, use a small stick-on note to label each size group for each fabric with the number and block location where it will be used.

Paper Foundations

Each block requires a paper foundation. One way to make these paper foundations is to photocopy the designs. Be sure to make all your copies on the same copying machine from the original design for each quilt. You should also check the accuracy of your photocopies against the originals. For a nominal fee, most copy shops will remove the binding of this book and three-hole punch the pages or spiral bind it to make using it on a copy machine even easier.

Another way to make these paper foundations is to use the Carol Doak Designer Edition, Version 3, of the Foundation Factory software. This software will permit you to print the designs from your PC and print multiples of the same design to a page when their size will permit this. See "Resources" on page 95 for order information and system requirements for this software.

The foundation piecing paper should hold up during the sewing process and be easy to remove when the top is complete. If in doubt, test your paper by sewing through it with a size 90/14 needle and a stitch length of 18 to 20 stitches per inch. If it tears as you sew, it is not strong enough. If it doesn't tear away easily when pulled after sewing, it is too strong. The paper does not need to be translucent. The light from your sewing machine is sufficient to see through the blank side of the paper to the lines on the other side. The Papers for Foundation Piecing from Martingale & Company work well for these projects (see "Resources" on page 95).

After you have made the necessary copies, cut out each block, leaving a generous ¼" from the outside line. To do this quickly and easily, staple the centers of up to four papers together, use your rotary cutter to trim the stapled foundations all at once (leaving your generous ¼" margin), then remove the staple.

PAPER-PIECING TECHNIQUES

WITH YOUR foundations copied and trimmed, and your fabric selected, cut, and labeled, you are ready to begin paper piecing your blocks. Always remember that the numbered and lined side of the foundation is the reverse (or mirror image) of the finished block. This often confuses beginners to paper piecing because they look at the lined side and try to think in reverse. The solution is to place your fabric pieces by looking through the blank side of the paper to the lines on the other side. This way, what you see is what you get, and you don't need to think in reverse.

Tracing paper has been used as the foundation for the block examples in our photographs so that you can see the lines through the blank side of the paper.

STEP-BY-STEP PAPER PIECING

1. Use a size 90/14 sewing machine needle, an open-toe presser foot for good visibility, and a stitch length of 18 to 20 stitches per inch. This is approximately 1.5 on a sewing machine that has a stitch length range of 0 to 5. The larger needle and smaller stitch length will allow you to remove the paper easily.
2. Using the light on your sewing machine, look through the blank side of the paper to place fabric piece #1 right side up over the area marked #1. Turn the paper over to make sure that it covers area #1 and extends at least ¼" beyond all seam lines. Pin into place.

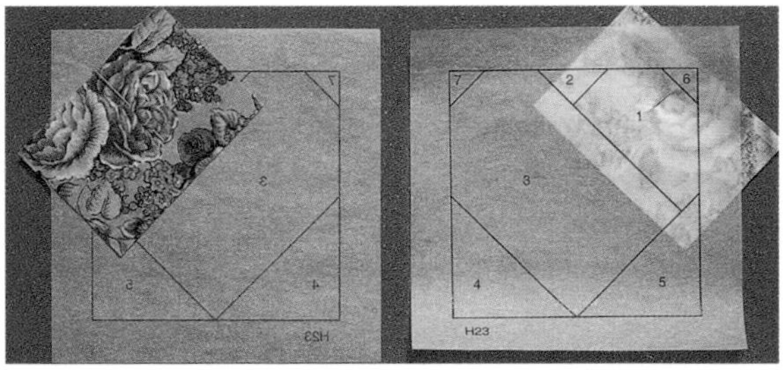

3. Place the edge of the postcard on the line between #1 and #2, and fold the paper back over the postcard to expose the excess fabric beyond the seam line.

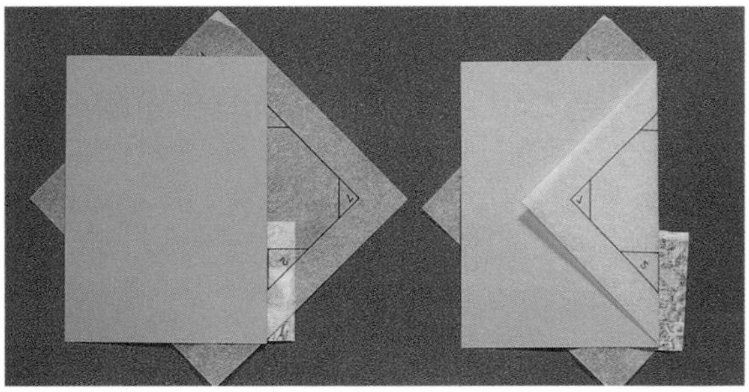

4. Place the Add-a-Quarter ruler on the fold, and trim the excess fabric ¼" from the fold. The lip on this ruler prevents it from slipping as you trim. If you prefer, you can trim by aligning the ¼" line on a rotary ruler with the fold.

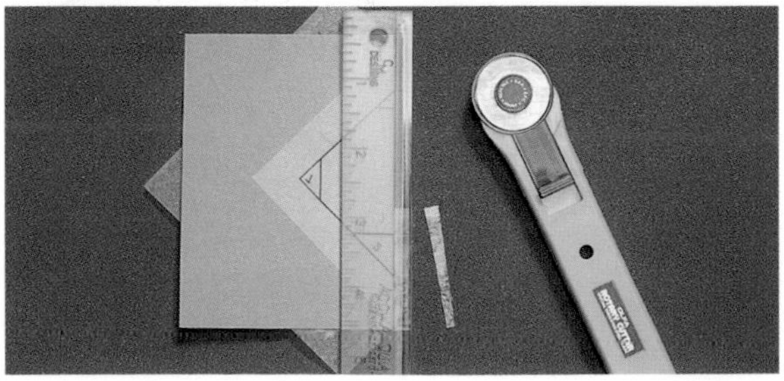

5. Looking through the blank side of the paper to the design on the other side, place piece #2 *right* side up over area #2. This is an important step. The reason you want to look through the blank side of the paper to position the next piece is to see how the fabric will appear after it is sewn and pressed open. Remember, what you see is what you get.

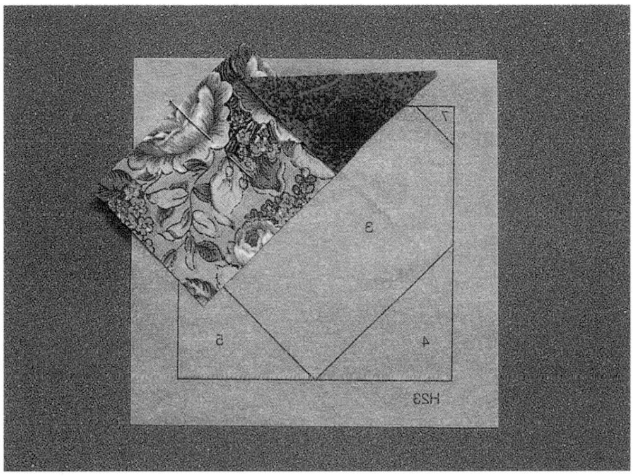

After piece #2 is properly positioned, flip it right sides together with the just-trimmed edge of piece #1. Looking through the blank side of the paper again, check that the end of piece #2 extends beyond the seam line of area #2 on the foundation.

If you are using cotton fabric, this piece should cling to piece #1, but you can pin piece #2 in place if you prefer. If you are using slippery fabrics such as satins, you must pin this piece in place.

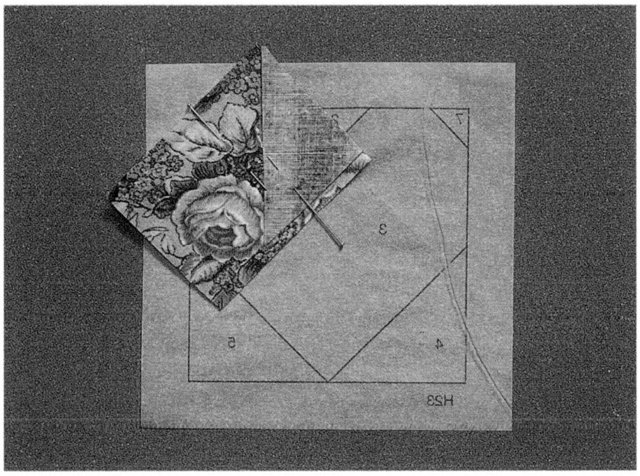

6. Place the foundation under the presser foot. Sew on the seam line between #1 and #2, beginning about ¼" to ½" before the seam and extending the stitching about the same distance beyond the seam end.

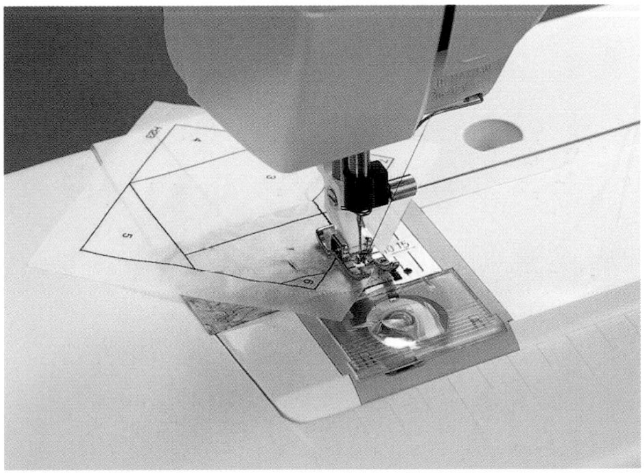

7. Clip the threads (see "Paper-Piecing Tips" on page 15 for a neat trick). Remove the pin and open piece #2. If you are using cotton fabrics, press with a dry iron on a cotton setting. If you are using heat-sensitive fabrics, use a pressing cloth or lower the temperature on the iron. Cover your ironing surface with a piece of scrap fabric to protect it from any ink that may transfer from the photocopies.

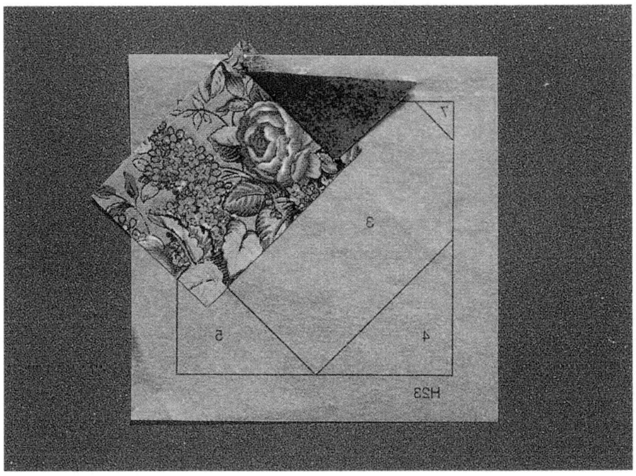

8. Place the edge of the postcard on the next line you will sew. This is where piece #3 adjoins the previous pieces. Fold the paper back across the postcard to expose the excess fabrics. If necessary, pull the stitches away from the foundation in order to fold the paper. Place the Add-a-Quarter ruler on the fold and trim ¼" from the fold, or use your rotary ruler as described previously.

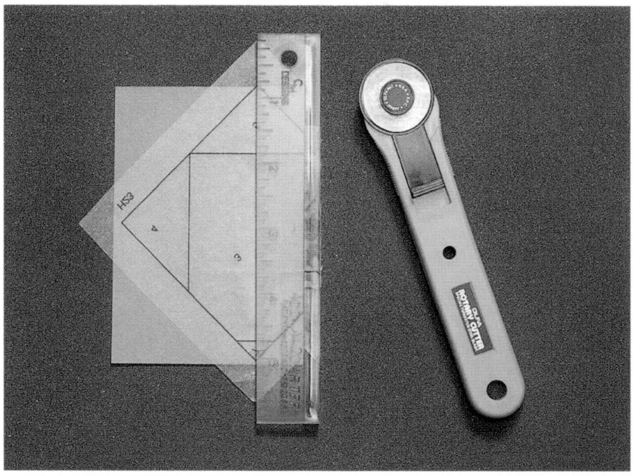

9. Place piece #3 *right* side up over area #3 to check for proper placement. Place the fabric right sides together with the just-trimmed edges of pieces #1 and #2. Note that the fabric extends on both sides for adequate seam allowances. Sew and press open.

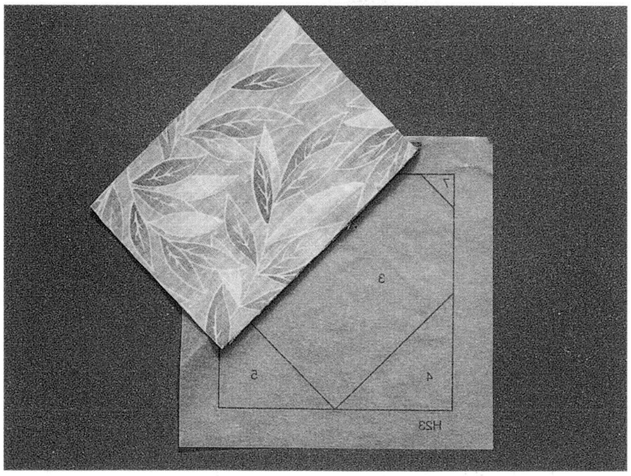

10. Continue with piece #4 by placing the edge of the postcard on the line between #3 and #4. Fold the paper back over the postcard and trim the excess fabric ¼" from the fold. Place piece #4 *right* side up over area #4 to check for proper placement, and then flip it right sides together along the just-trimmed edge. Align the corner of the fabric triangle with the corner of the triangle printed on the foundation. Sew and press open.

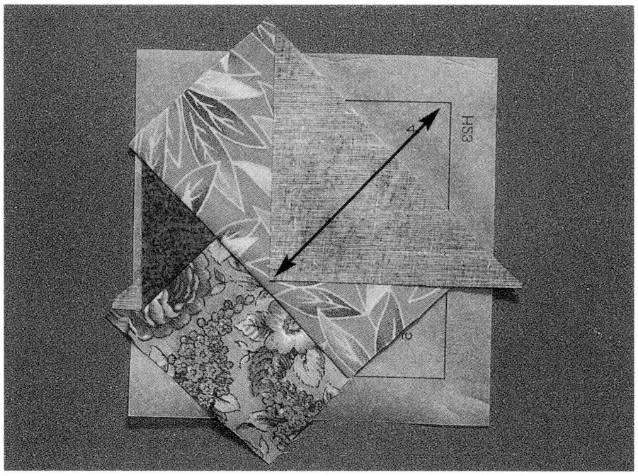

11. Continue in the same manner until all the pieces have been added.

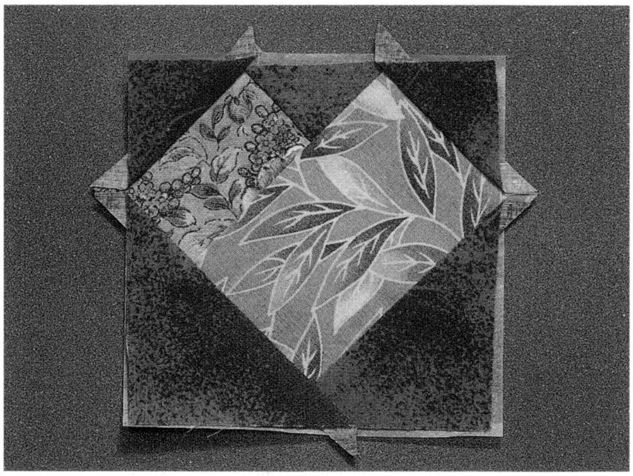

12. Using the rotary ruler, align the ¼" line on the outside sewing line and trim the foundation ¼" from the sewing line on all sides. Don't remove the paper. That will come later.

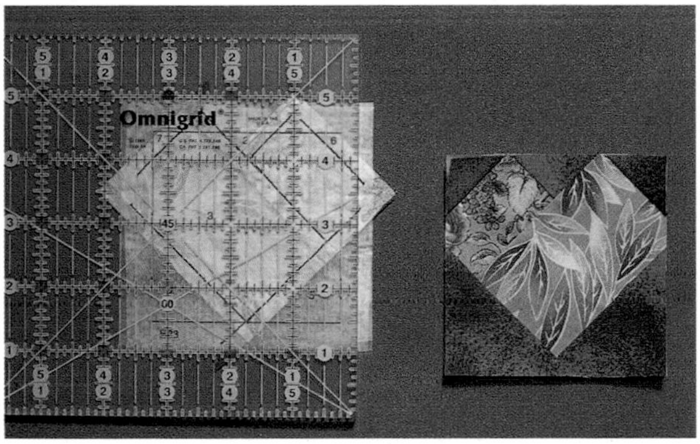

Paper-Piecing Tips

- Set up a pressing area next to your sewing machine. You can lower an ironing board to make access more convenient. Cover your ironing surface with a piece of scrap fabric, as the heat may cause some of the ink from the copies to transfer.
- Use a small travel iron set on a cotton setting. If you are using heat-sensitive fabrics, adjust the iron temperature accordingly.
- Sew similar blocks in assembly-line fashion without cutting the threads in-between until later. This will speed up the paper-piecing process.
- One of my students recently shared a trick that saves me a lot of time clipping threads. With the paper side facing up, pull up on the top thread to pull the bobbin thread up slightly. Using sharp thread clippers, clip close to the surface of the foundation. Most of the time you will be able to cut the bobbin thread at the same time you are cutting the top threads. Give it a try and you may just find that it saves you time too.

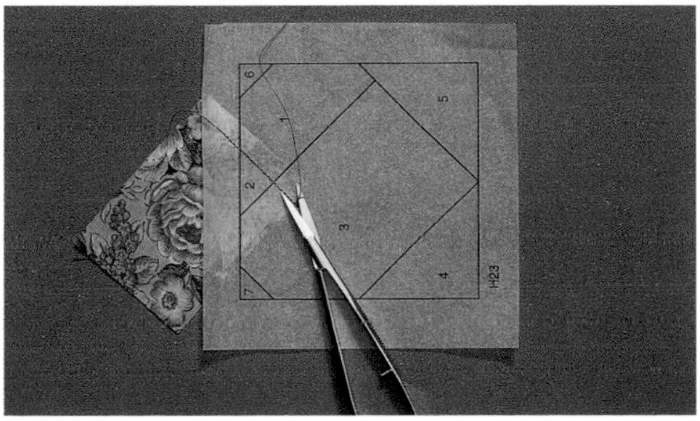

- If it becomes necessary to repair a torn foundation, use Scotch brand removable tape. Do not touch the iron directly to the tape.
- If it becomes necessary to remove a line of stitching, place a piece of Scotch brand removable tape on the stitching line to be removed. Pull the top fabric piece back to expose the thread. Lightly touch the point of the Olfa rotary point cutter to the threads, keeping tension on the fabric as the threads are cut. This method of removing the stitches not only goes quickly, but the tape also provides a good foundation for resewing the seam line.

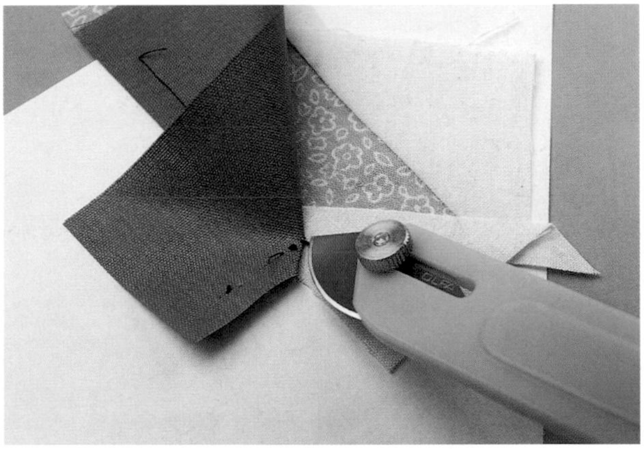

- If you should unknowingly run out of bobbin thread while sewing and need to restitch the same line, use the tape along the seam line so the foundation won't tear when sewn again.

Pieced Units

Some of the designs have pieced units that are made up of fabric pieces sewn together prior to adding them to the foundation. Pieced units may have one seam or two. Where a pieced unit is required, one number has been assigned to the entire unit and hatch marks have been used to indicate the seam(s) to be pieced prior to adding the unit to the foundation.

For example, to make several pieced units such as piece #6 in the tree block (T22) for "Old MacDonald's Farm" quilt (see page 46), sew the required strips into a strip unit as shown. Press the seams and cut the strip unit into the required number of 1¾"-wide segments.

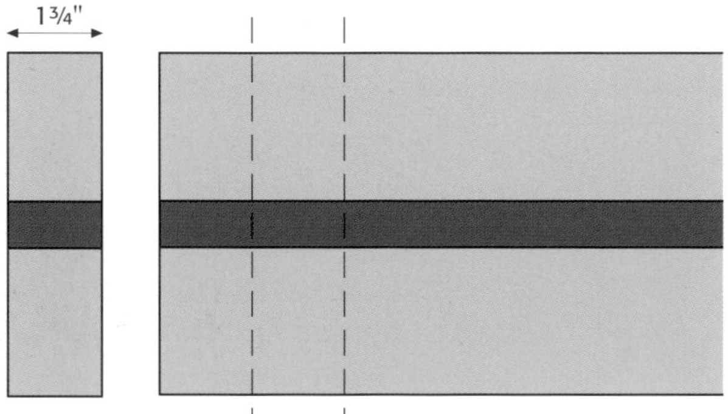

Cut 24 units.

When it is time to add piece #6, look through the blank side, align the seam lines of the trunk with the seam lines on the paper, and pin in place. Stitch and press piece #6 open. With the vertical seams straight, machine baste the seam allowance along the edge of the block for about an inch so that the pieced unit won't move when the block is joined to other blocks.

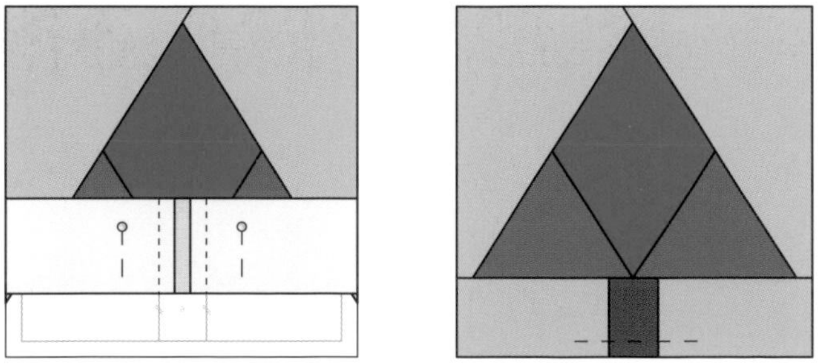

Machine baste trunk straight.

When only a few pieced units are needed, such as the pieced units for some of the blocks in "The Night Train" (see page 55), sew the fabric pieces together as illustrated in the traditional fashion. Use a ¼" seam allowance.

Sometimes it is easier to create your pieced unit on the foundation prior to paper piecing the block, pretending that they are pieces #1 and #2. I used this approach for the #6 and #7 pieced units in the Teddy Bear block (P56D). Position the teddy bear fabric for piece #6 as if it were piece #1 and pin in place. Fold the paper back on the line with the hatch marks and trim the excess fabric ¼" from the fold. Next, position the background fabric triangle as if it were piece #2, and sew on the seam line with the hatch marks, directly on the foundation. Press open. Fold the paper back along the line where pieced unit #6 meets the #1/#5 line, and trim the just sewn pieces ¼" from the fold. Place a piece of Scotch brand removable tape along the just-sewn line and carefully remove the pieced unit. Follow this same procedure for the #7 pieced unit.

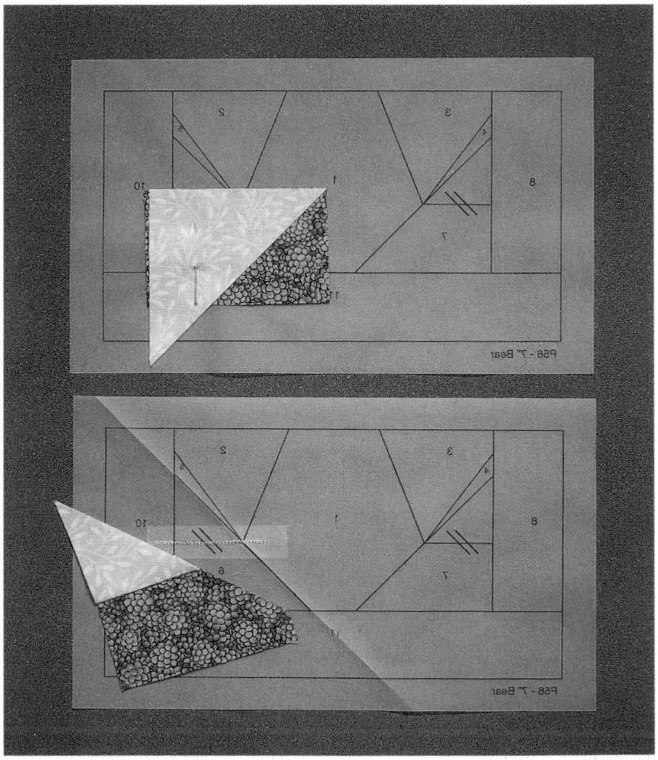

When it is time to add the #6 pieced unit, place a pin in the sewn seam line of the pieced unit ¼" in from the edge and then in the seam line of the paper. This will correctly position the seam.

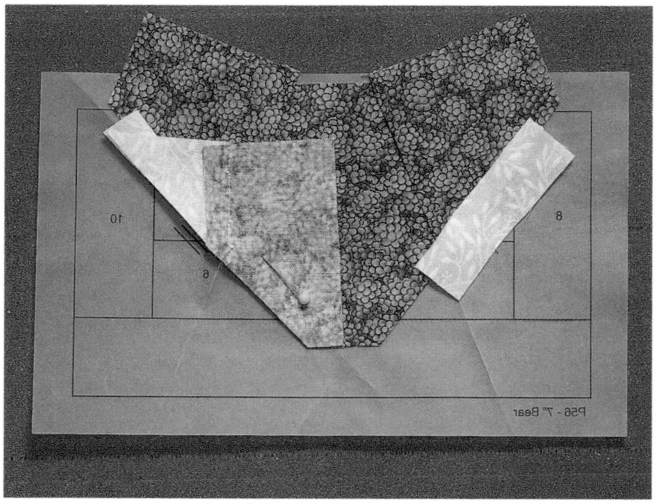

Secure the pieced unit in place with another pin and sew. Press open and machine baste the pieced unit to the paper so that the horizontal seam is straight. Follow the same procedure for the #7 pieced unit.

Assembly Techniques

Once the components of your baby quilt have been made, you are ready to assemble them according to the quilt plan.

Block Assembly

After the blocks or block sections have been paper pieced, the next step is to join them. In the following photographs, unpieced foundations are used for illustration purposes. Follow these simple procedures for sure success!

Place the trimmed blocks right sides together and pin away from the seam line you will be sewing. First, machine baste the seam at the beginning, any matching points, and the end. When you have completed one area, move the block to the next area. You don't need to cut the threads until later.

Next, remove the pins and open the unit to check for a good match. If you want to fix any part, simply clip the basting thread from the bobbin side and remove it. Pin and machine baste as before. When everything is as it should be, sew the blocks together with the smaller stitch.

This basting technique is well worth your time! In the following photo, the top and bottom unpieced foundations of the basket block are machine basted at the beginning, middle, and end of the seam line, as well as at the handle areas.

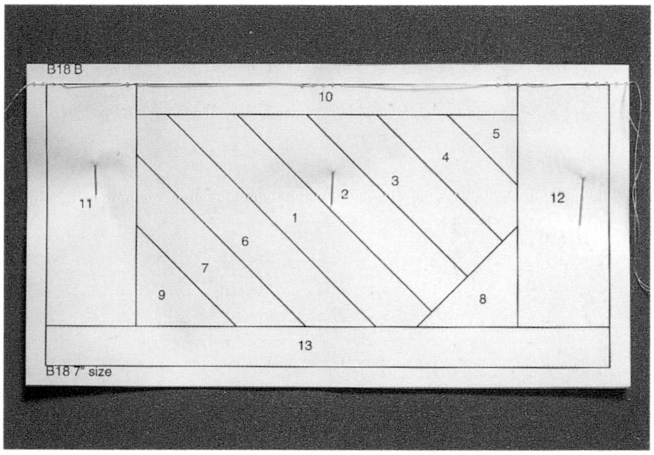

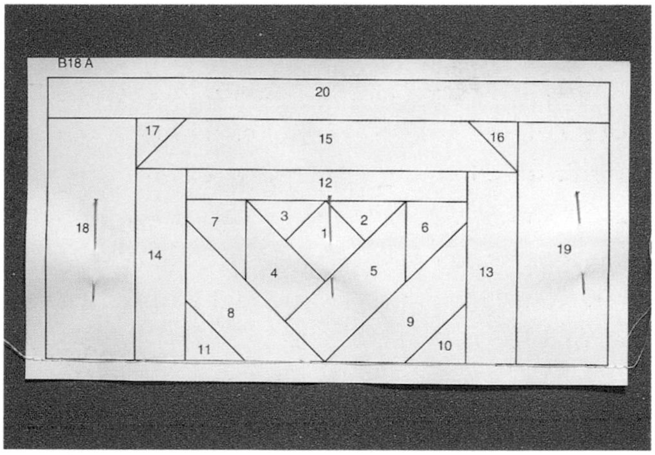

Angled Sections

In the Teddy Bear block, sections P56A and P56B are joined along an angled seam rather than a vertical or horizontal seam. To make sure these angled pieces are correctly aligned, place the pieces on top of each other and insert a pin straight through both ends of the seam lines that need to match. Don't bring the points up through the pieces. Instead, pin the sections together with additional pins, as in the following photograph.

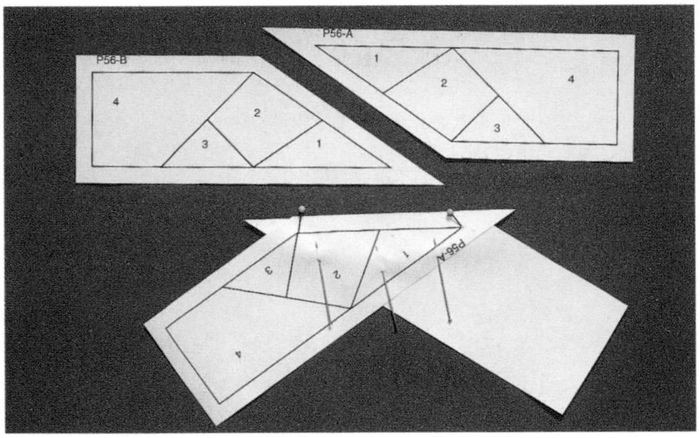

Set-in Seams

To be honest, I never thought I would be describing how easy it is to sew set-in seams, but paper piecing makes this easy. The baby blocks, P64 and P65, have set-in pieces and will serve to illustrate just how easy this process is. The two bottom sections are joined in P64 to produce the set-in seam to which the top is joined. The P65 block has a one-piece lower section.

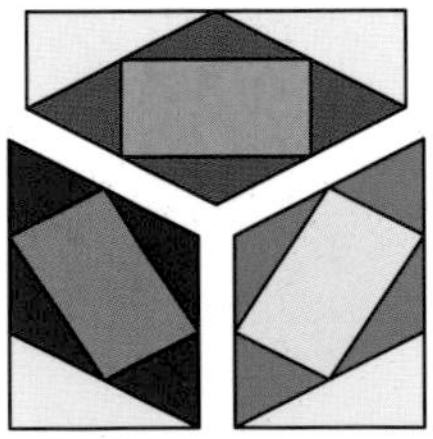

P64 sections

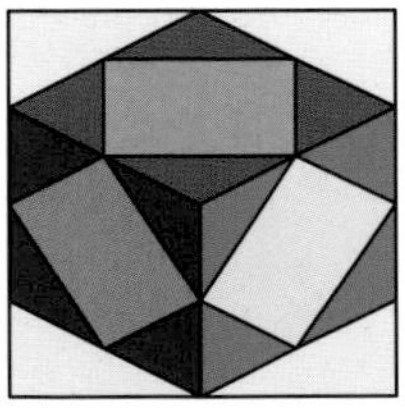

P64

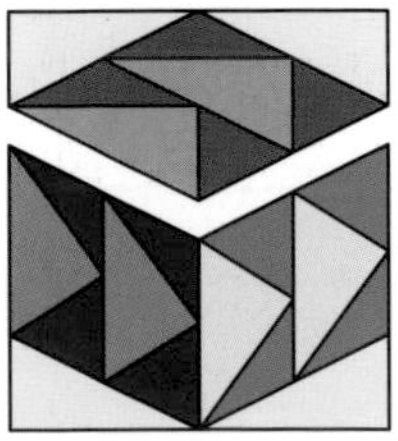

P65 sections

P65

Joining sections for P64

1. Join P64A and P64B in the usual manner, but start at the beginning of the line at the top of #2. Don't sew through the seam allowance at the top. Sew to the end of the pieces, through the seam allowances beyond #3 pieces. Press seam allowances toward P64A.

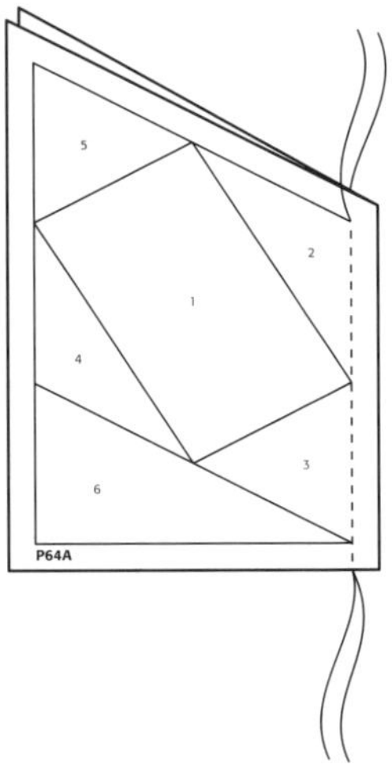

2. Insert straight pins vertically at the end of the line to match the #3/#4 side of P64C to the #5/#2 side of P64B. Add additional pins away from the seam line.
3. Starting at the outside edge, machine baste a short distance at the beginning, middle, and the end of the line at the center of the set-in piece. Don't sew beyond the center point (the triangle point at piece #3).

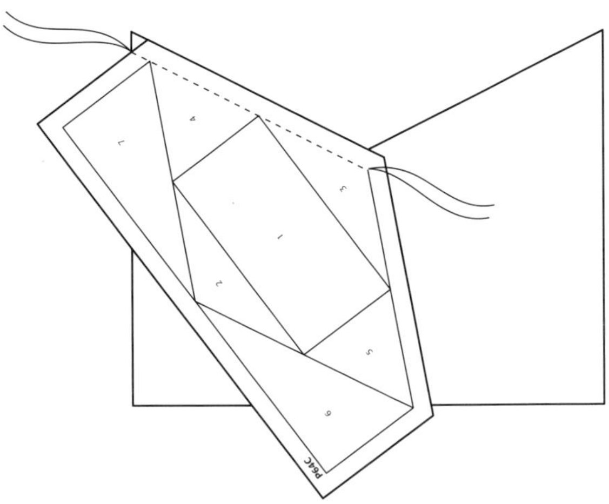

4. Check for a good match. Switch to a smaller stitch and sew to the center, stopping at the end of the line with the needle in the down position. Pivot the pieces on the needle, pin the remaining side at the end and machine baste. Check for a good match. With a smaller stitch, sew from the outside to the center. Press seam allowances toward the bottom sections.

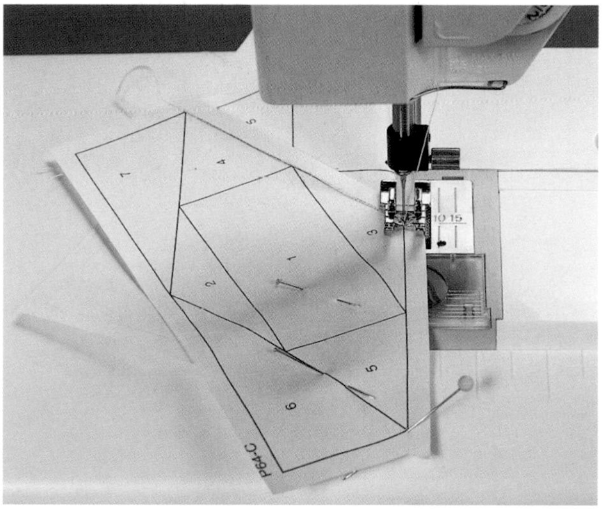

Joining sections for P65

1. Make a slit in the seam allowance to the seam line at the center of P65B where #6, #7, and #9 meet.

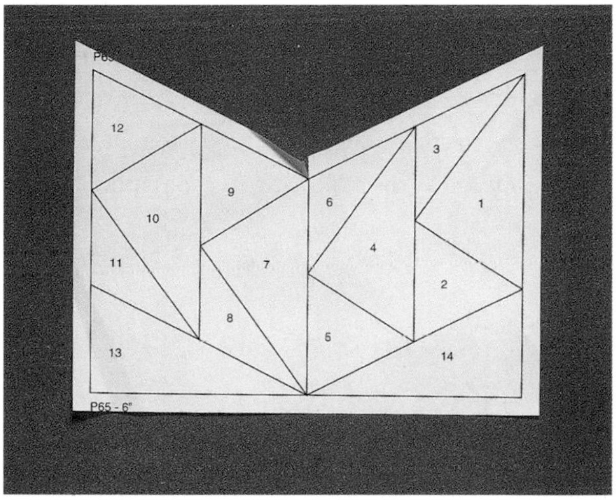

2. Follow the same procedure for sewing the set-in seam as described for P64, beginning with step 2.

QUILT-TOP ASSEMBLY

WHEN SEWING rows of blocks together, join the blocks as previously described and press the seam allowance in opposite directions from row to row so that the seams will lock in place. Always machine baste and check for a good match before sewing the rows together with a smaller stitch.

Begin joining blocks for a medallion style quilt in the center of the quilt, and add blocks and borders in a logical fashion. Pin fabric borders in place. With the foundation blocks on top, machine baste at beginnings and ends, and about every 6" or where a point is formed. Check for accuracy before sewing with the smaller stitch. When sewing fabric to fabric, increase the stitch length to twelve stitches per inch.

When the top is complete, remove the paper. Start at the outside edge of the quilt and pull against the stitches. This is one of those activities that requires little concentration; save it for when you're watching TV or just relaxing. Use tweezers to remove the bits of paper from intersecting seam allowances.

BABY QUILTS

BE SURE to read the front portion of this book through once before beginning a baby quilt, as it contains valuable information and tips to assist you. The directions for each quilt include a quilt plan that shows you the layout of the blocks and borders. The sizes on the quilt plans for the border and setting pieces indicate the cut size.

Yardage requirements are provided for each quilt. I have indicated where nondirectional fabric is suggested; unless noted otherwise, directional or nondirectional fabric will work equally well. If you'd like to add a sleeve, add 12" to the yardage requirement for the backing fabric.

The finished paper-pieced blocks are shown with their corresponding fabric placements and the number of blocks you will need to make. As in my previous paper-piecing books, I have numbered the block designs with the letter of the category, such as B for baskets, and the next consecutive number in each category. The full-sized paper-piecing designs are provided on pages 63–94. Remember that the foundation piecing designs are the reverse images of the finished block designs.

Border and binding strips are cut across the width of the fabric. Cut these and any setting pieces first if you are using the same fabric for the blocks. That way, you can use the leftover yardage to cut the smaller pieces for the blocks. When a portion of a strip was needed for binding, I rounded up to a whole strip.

The cutting lists indicate the number of pieces you will need to cut, the sizes to cut from each fabric, and where those fabrics are to be used. In creating the cutting lists, I often rounded up to larger pieces in order to simplify the cutting process. When you see this symbol ⧅ in the cutting list, cut the squares once diagonally to yield two half-square triangles. When you see this symbol ⊠, cut the squares twice diagonally to yield four quarter-square triangles (see page 10). Remember to label each group of cut fabrics with the number and block where they'll be used, so that you will know which fabric to use when paper piecing the blocks.

Following the cutting lists, you'll find tips for making some quilts.

So, your game plan is as follows:

1. Read the front portion of the book.
2. Choose the first quilt you'd like to make.
3. Choose the fabrics you'd like to use.
4. Cut the border, binding, and setting pieces.
5. Cut the fabric pieces in the cutting list and label them.
6. Make the foundations indicated and trim them a generous ¼" from the outside line.
7. Make the paper-pieced blocks indicated using the fabric placements indicated.
8. Assemble and sew the blocks and setting pieces according to the quilt plan.
9. Remove the paper, sandwich your quilt, quilt as desired, and bind the quilt.
10. Put a label on the back of the quilt and give your gift to your special baby.

Teddy Bear Love

By Carol Doak, 2000, Windham, New Hampshire, 35½" x 42½". This huggable little quilt combines cute bow-tied teddy bears and colorful red hearts set in an alternating block fashion. The quilted heart border continues the lovable theme. Machine quilted by Ellen Peters.

MATERIALS

42"-wide fabric

- ⅞ yd. paisley for outer border and binding
- 1 yd. beige for inner border and blocks (nondirectional)
- ⅛ yd. red-and-black check
- ½ yd. white-and-red print
- ⅛ yd. red #1
- ¼ yd. red #2
- ¼ yd. red #3
- ⅛ yd. red #4
- ⅜ yd. brown (nondirectional)
- 1⅜ yds. for backing
- 39" x 46" piece of batting

CUTTING FOR BORDERS AND BINDING

Fabric	No. of Pieces	Dimensions	Location
Paisley	4	4" x 35½"	Outer border
	4	2" x 40"	Binding
Beige	2	4" x 28½"	Inner side border
	2	4" x 21½"	Inner top and bottom border

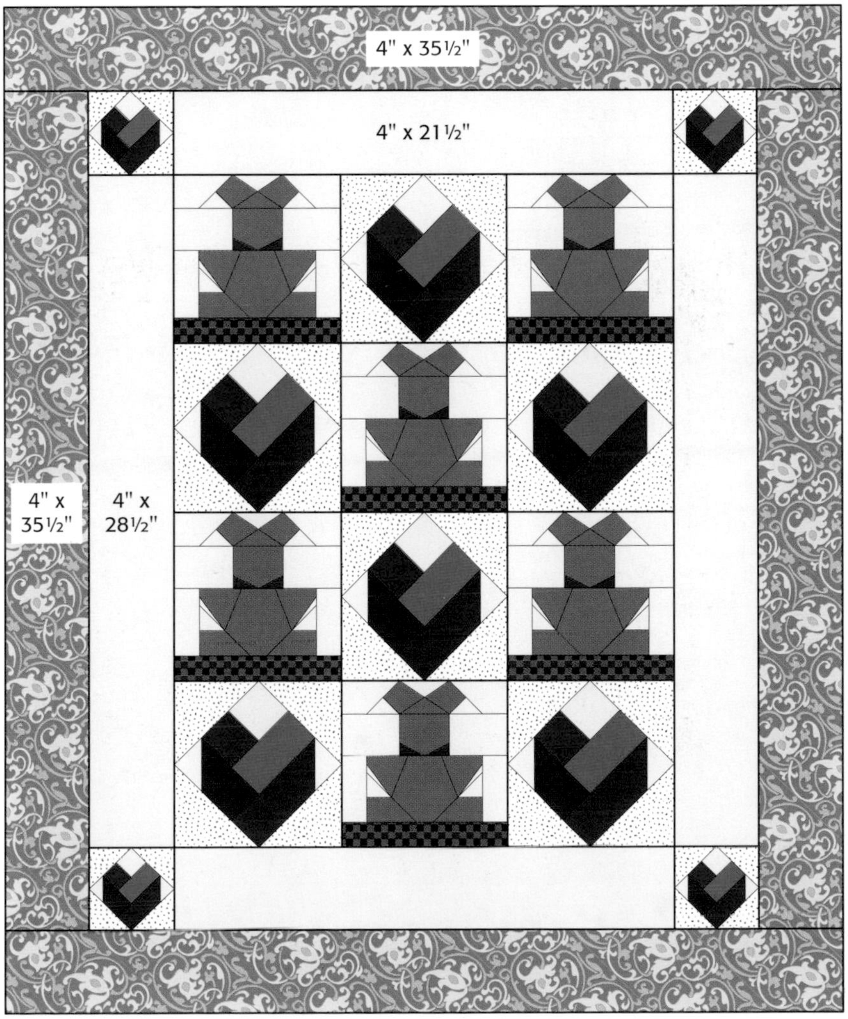

Measurements in quilt plan are cut sizes.

CUTTING FOR BLOCKS

Fabric	No. of Pieces	Dimensions	Location Numbers	Block
Beige	3	3¾" x 3¾" ⊠	6, 7	H19 large
	3	3" x 3" ⊠	3	P56A, P56B
	6	2¾" x 2¾" ⧅	6, 7	P56D*
	2	2¾" x 2¾" ⊠	6, 7	H19 small
	6	2½" x 2½"	1	H19 large
	12	2½" x 3¾"	4	P56A, P56B**
	12	2½" x 3¼"	4, 5	P56C
	12	1¾" x 3½"	8, 9	P56D
	4	1½" x 1½"	1	H19 small
	6	1½" x 3"	1	P56A
	12	1" x 2½"	4, 5	P56D
Red/black check	6	1¾" x 8"	10	P56D
White/red print	12	4¾" x 4¾" ⧅	8, 9, 10, 11	H19 large
	8	3" x 3" ⧅	8, 9, 10, 11	H19 small
Red #1	6	2¼" x 4"	3	H19 large
	4	1½" x 2¼"	3	H19 small
Red #2	6	2½" x 2½"	2	H19 large
	4	1½" x 1½"	2	H19 small
	12	1½" x 2¼"	2, 3	P56C
Red #3	6	2¼" x 5¾"	5	H19 large
	4	1½" x 3¼"	5	H19 small
Red #4	6	2¼" x 4"	4	H19 large
	4	1½" x 2½"	4	H19 small
Brown	6	3½" x 3½"	1	P56D
	18	2½" x 3"	1	P56C
			2, 3	P56D
	12	2" x 2½"	2	P56A, P56B
	12	1¾" x 2¾"	6, 7	P56D*
	6	1½" x 3"	1	P56B

* See pages 16–17 for directions on making the #6 and #7 pieced units on the P56D foundations.

** See tip at right for cutting angled pieces.

Make the following paper-pieced blocks.

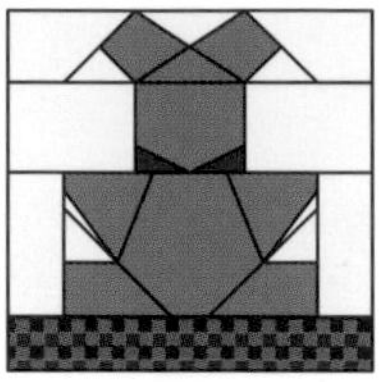
P56
Make 6
(page 64).

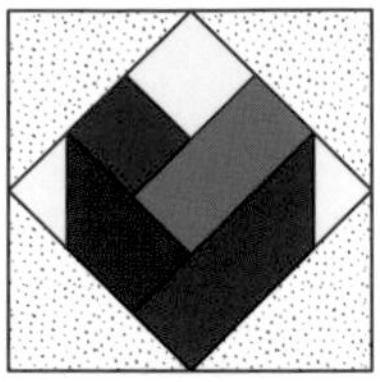
H19
Make 6 large
(page 63).

H19
Make 4 small
(page 65).

TIP

To cut the 45° angle for piece #4 in P56A and P56B, place two rectangles of fabric right sides together and position the rotary ruler as shown to cut the end of the pieces at a 45° angle. Repeat with the remaining pieces.

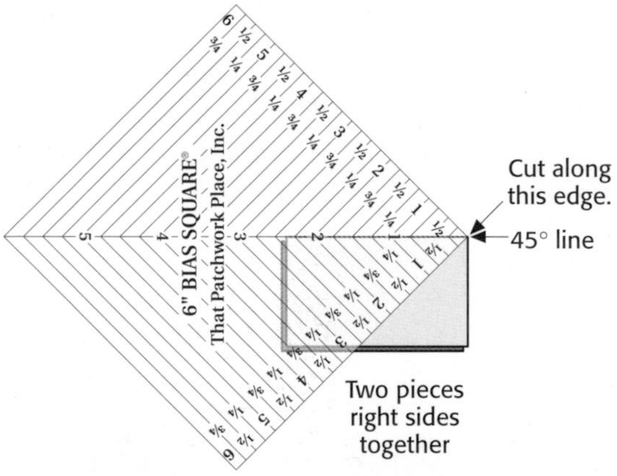

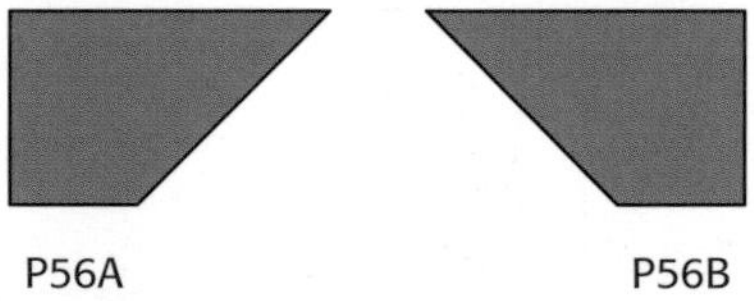

Before joining P56A and P56B, see page 18 on joining angled sections.

Up, Up, and Away

By Carol Doak, 2000, Windham, New Hampshire, 32½" x 38½". What child wouldn't imagine floating among the quilted clouds in one of these colorful hot air balloons? Machine quilted by Ellen Peters.

Materials

42"-wide fabric

- ⅞ yd. dark blue for inner border, outer border, and binding
- 1¼ yds. light blue for middle border and blocks (nondirectional)
- ⅛ yd. white
- ⅛ yd. black
- ¾ yd. total assorted solids
- 1¼ yd. for backing
- 36" x 42" piece of batting

Cutting for Borders and Binding

Fabric	No. of Pieces	Dimensions	Location
Dark blue	2	2½" x 34½"	Outer side border
	2	2½" x 32½"	Outer top and bottom border
	4	2½" x 20½"	Inner border
	4	2" x 40"	Binding
Light blue	4	5½" x 8½"	Middle top and bottom border
	4	4½" x 10"	Middle side border

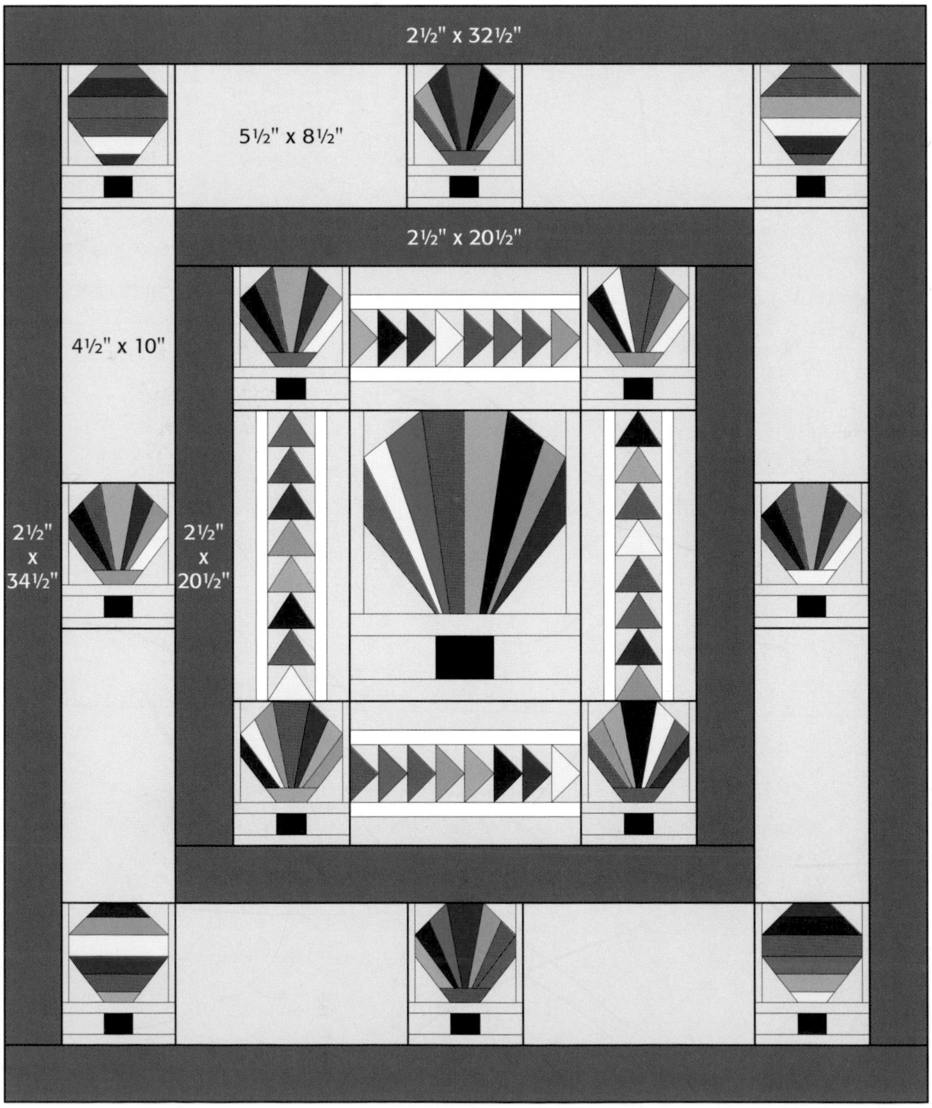

Measurements in quilt plan are cut sizes.

Cutting for Blocks

Fabric	No. of Pieces	Dimensions	Location Numbers	Block
Light blue	12	3" x 3" ⧅	9, 10	P58A
			7, 8	P59A
	2	2¾" x 5"	11, 12	P57A
	44	2½" x 2½" ⧅	All small triangles	PB12, PB13
			11, 12	P58A
			9, 10	P59A
	2	2¼" x 3¾"	2, 3	P57B
	2	2" x 3½"	9, 10	P57A
	4	1¾" x 9"	27, 28	PB12
	4	1½" x 11"	27, 28	PB13
	2	1½" x 9"	4, 5	P57B
	24	1½" x 2¼"	2, 3	P58B, P59B
	2	1¼" x 8"	13, 14	P57A
	48	1" x 5"	4, 5	P58B, P59B
			13, 14	P58A
			11, 12	P59A
White	4	1" x 9"	25, 26	PB12
	4	1" x 11"	25, 26	PB13
Black	1	2¼" x 2¾"	1	P57B
	12	1½" x 1¾"	1	P58B, P59B
Assorted solids	8	3¾" x 3¾" ⊠	All large triangles	PB12, PB13
	4	2¼" x 8"	1, 2, 3, 4	P57A
	8	2" x 4"	1	P58A
	4	1¾" x 7½"	5, 6, 7, 8	P57A
	52	1¼" x 4"	2, 3, 4, 5	P58A
			1 through 5	P59A
	28	1" x 3½"	6, 7, 8	P58A
			6	P59A

Make the following paper-pieced blocks and borders.

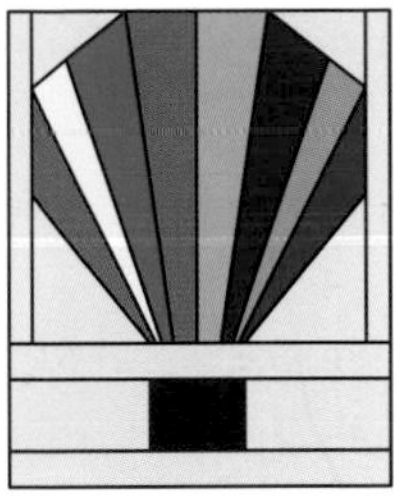

P57
Make 1
(pages 66, 67).

P58
Make 8
(page 68).

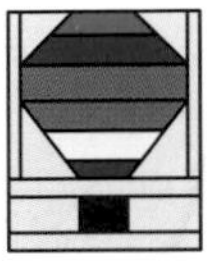

P59
Make 4
(page 69).

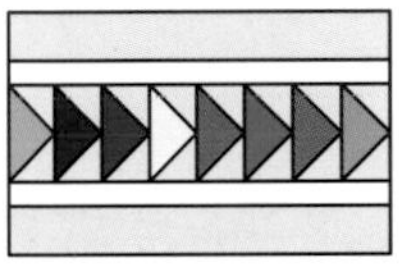

PB12
Make 2 (page 70).

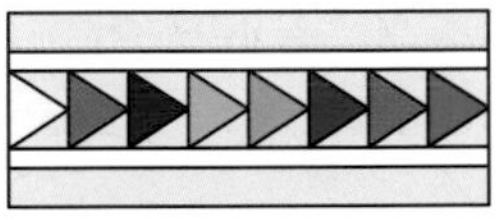

PB13
Make 2 (page 71).

Tips

- Layer the assorted solid colors to cut multiple pieces at one time.
- When paper piecing long strips, pin them in place before sewing.

Crazy About You

By Carol Doak, 2000, Windham, New Hampshire, 30½" x 30½". A variety of gold and neutral dressy fabrics are combined in crazy patch hearts and borders in this little medallion-style quilt, perfect for a special christening day. Delicate small quilted hearts create a delightful detail. Machine quilted by Ellen Peters.

Materials

42"-wide fabric

- ¾ yd. medium beige for outer border, inner border, and binding
- ⅜ yd. light beige for middle border
- ⅜ yd. white for corner squares and blocks
- ¾ yd. assorted beige/gold fabrics
- 1 yd. for backing
- 34" x 34" piece of batting

Cutting for Borders, Binding, and Setting Pieces

Fabric	No. of Pieces	Dimensions	Location
Medium beige	2	3½" x 30½"	Outer top and bottom border
	2	3½" x 24½"	Outer side border
	2	1" x 8½"	Inner top and bottom border
	2	1" x 7½"	Inner side border
	3	2" x 40"	Binding
Light beige	4	4½" x 16½"	Middle border
White	4	4½" x 4½"	Corner squares

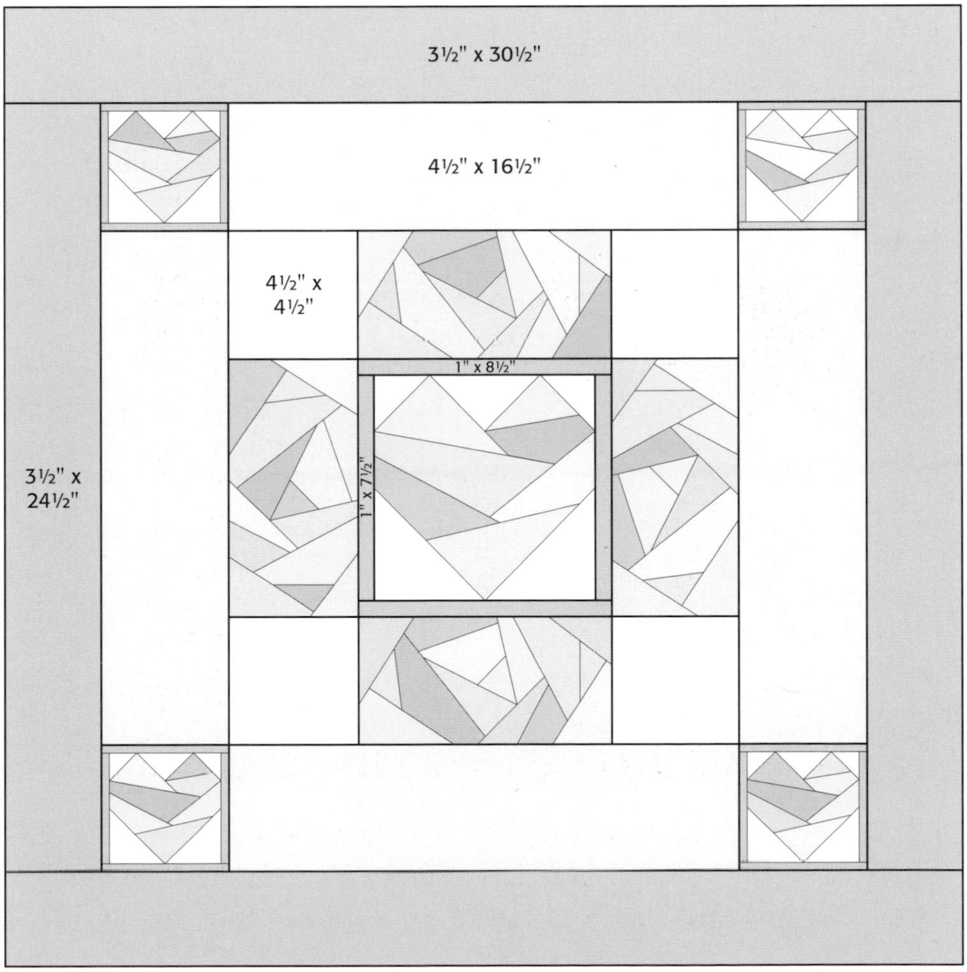

Measurements in quilt plan are cut sizes.

Cutting for Blocks

Fabric	No. of Pieces	Dimensions	Location Numbers	Block
Medium beige	16	1" x 5"	13, 14, 15, 16	H21
White	1	4¾" x 4¾" ⧅	9, 10	H20
	1	3¼" x 3¼" ⊠	1	H21
	5	3" x 3" ⧅	11, 12	H20
			9, 10	H21
	1	2½" x 4½"	1	H20
	4	2" x 2" ⧅	11, 12	H21
Beiges/golds	7	3" x 7"	2 through 8	H20*
	28	1½" x 3½"	2 through 8	H21*
	60	2¼" x 5"	1 through 15	PB14*

* To simplify the cutting for the crazy patches, I cut the same size piece for the largest needed area for each block.

Make the following paper-pieced blocks and borders.

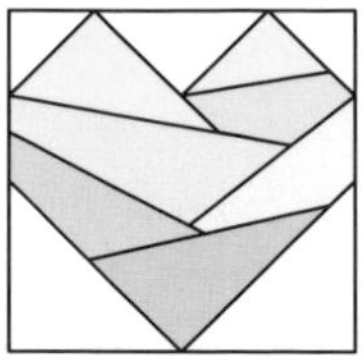

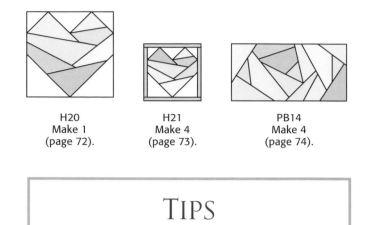

H20
Make 1
(page 72).

H21
Make 4
(page 73).

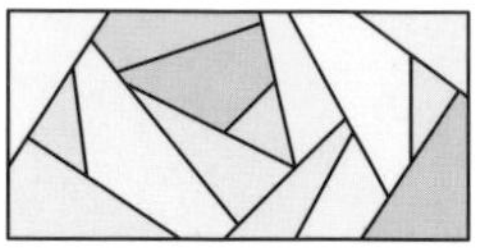

PB14
Make 4
(page 74).

Tips

- The silks and metallic gold fabrics are slippery. Pin these pieces in place before sewing.
- Use a pressing cloth for heat-sensitive fabrics.

A Blue and Yellow Basket

By Carol Doak, 2000, Windham, New Hampshire, 39½" x 39½". The nursery rhyme that begins "A tisket, a tasket, a blue and yellow basket," was the inspiration for combining flower-filled baskets surrounded by picket fences. A pretty quilt design fills the spaces between the star points. Machine quilted by Ellen Peters.

Materials

42"-wide fabric

- 1¼ yds. dark blue #1 for outer border, inner corner squares, binding, and blocks
- ½ yd. yellow for inner border, outer corner squares, and blocks
- 1 yd. white
- ¼ yd. medium blue
- ⅛ yd. dark blue #2
- ⅛ yd. dark blue #3
- ⅛ yd. green
- 1¼ yds. for backing
- 43" x 43" piece of batting

Cutting for Borders, Binding, and Setting Pieces

Fabric	No. of Pieces	Dimensions	Location
Dark blue #1	4	4" x 32½"	Outer border
	4	4" x 4"	Inner corner squares
	5	2" x 40"	Binding
Yellow	2	2½" x 32½"	Inner top and bottom border
	2	2½" x 28½"	Inner side border
	4	4" x 4"	Outer corner squares

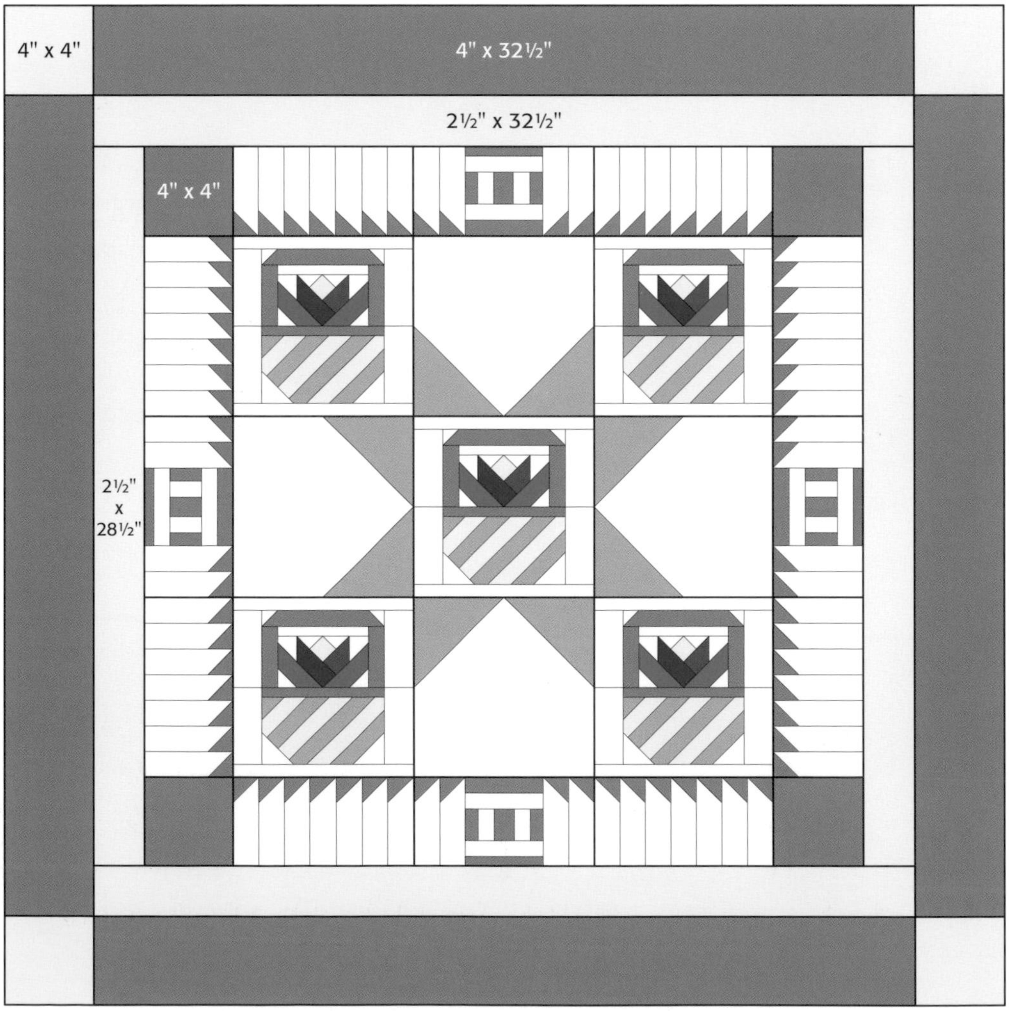

Measurements in quilt plan are cut sizes.

Cutting for Blocks

Fabric	No. of Pieces	Dimensions	Location Numbers	Block
Dark blue #1	36	2¼" x 2¼"	even numbers	P60, P61
			11, 13, 15, 17	P62
	10	1¼" x 5¾"	15	B18A
			10	B18B
	18	1¼" x 3½"	13, 14	B18A
			8, 9	P62
	12	1½" x 2"	1, 3, 5	P62
Yellow	15	1¼" x 4½"	2, 4, 6	B18B
	5	1½" x 1½"	1	B18A
White	4	7¾" x 7¾"	1	G90
	5	2½" x 2½"	8, 9	B18B
	15	2" x 2"	2, 3, 10, 11, 16, 17	B18A
	18	1½" x 2"	6, 7	B18A
			2, 4	P62
	92	1¾" x 4¼"	odd numbers	P60, P61
			10, 12, 14, 16	P62
			18, 19	B18A
			11, 12	B18B
	10	1¼" x 8"	20	B18A
			13	B18B
	8	1¼" x 3½"	6, 7	P62
	5	1" x 4½"	12	B18A
Medium blue	4	4¾" x 4¾"	2, 3	G90
	3	2" x 2"	5	B18B
	15	1¼" x 4¾"	1, 3, 7	B18B
Dark blue #2	5	1¼" x 3"	5	B18A
Dark blue #3	5	1¼" x 2"	4	B18A
Green	10	1½" x 3½"	8, 9	B18A

Make the following paper-pieced blocks.

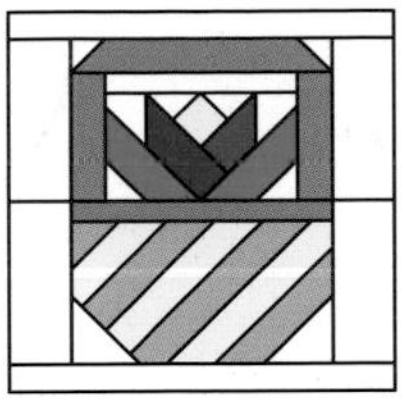

B18
Make 5
(page 75).

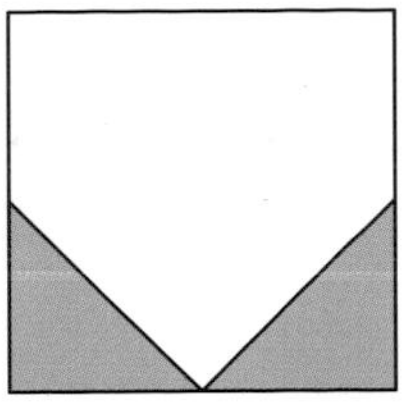

G90
Make 4
(page 76).

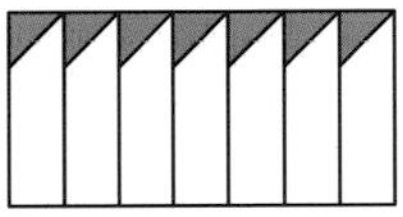

P60
Make 4
(page 77).

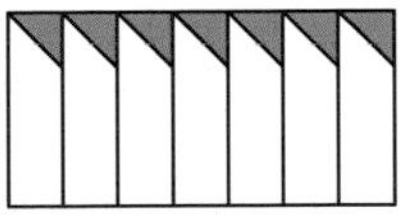

P61
Make 4
(page 77).

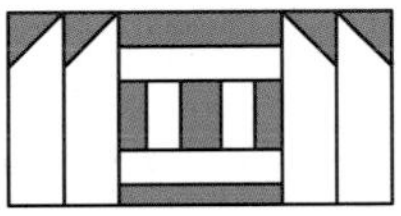

P62
Make 4
(page 73).

Tip

Don't forget to use the basting technique to check for a good match before joining the top and bottom basket sections (see page 17).

My Valentine

By Carol Doak, 2000, Windham, New Hampshire, 40½" x 40½". This medallion-style quilt features two heart designs with the smaller of the two used in a checkerboard fashion in the border. Although I used shades of pink, with a little girl in mind, this theme of love could be made using neutral or little boy colors. Machine quilted by Ellen Peters.

Materials

42"-wide fabric

- 1 yd. fuchsia #1 for outer border, binding, setting squares, and blocks
- ¾ yd. white for inner and middle borders
- ⅛ yd. fuchsia #2
- ⅓ yd. fuchsia #3
- ⅛ yd. fuchsia #4
- ⅓ yd. fuchsia #5
- ¾ yd. pink (nondirectional)
- 1¼ yds. for backing
- 44" x 44" piece of batting

Cutting for Borders, Binding, and Setting Pieces

Fabric	No. of Pieces	Dimensions	Location
Fuchsia #1	2	2½" x 40½"	Outer top and bottom border
	2	2½" x 36½"	Outer side border
	24	3½" x 3½"	Setting squares
	5	2" x 40"	Binding
White	4	3½" x 30½"	Middle border
	2	3½" x 18½"	Inner top and bottom border
	2	3½" x 12½"	Inner side border

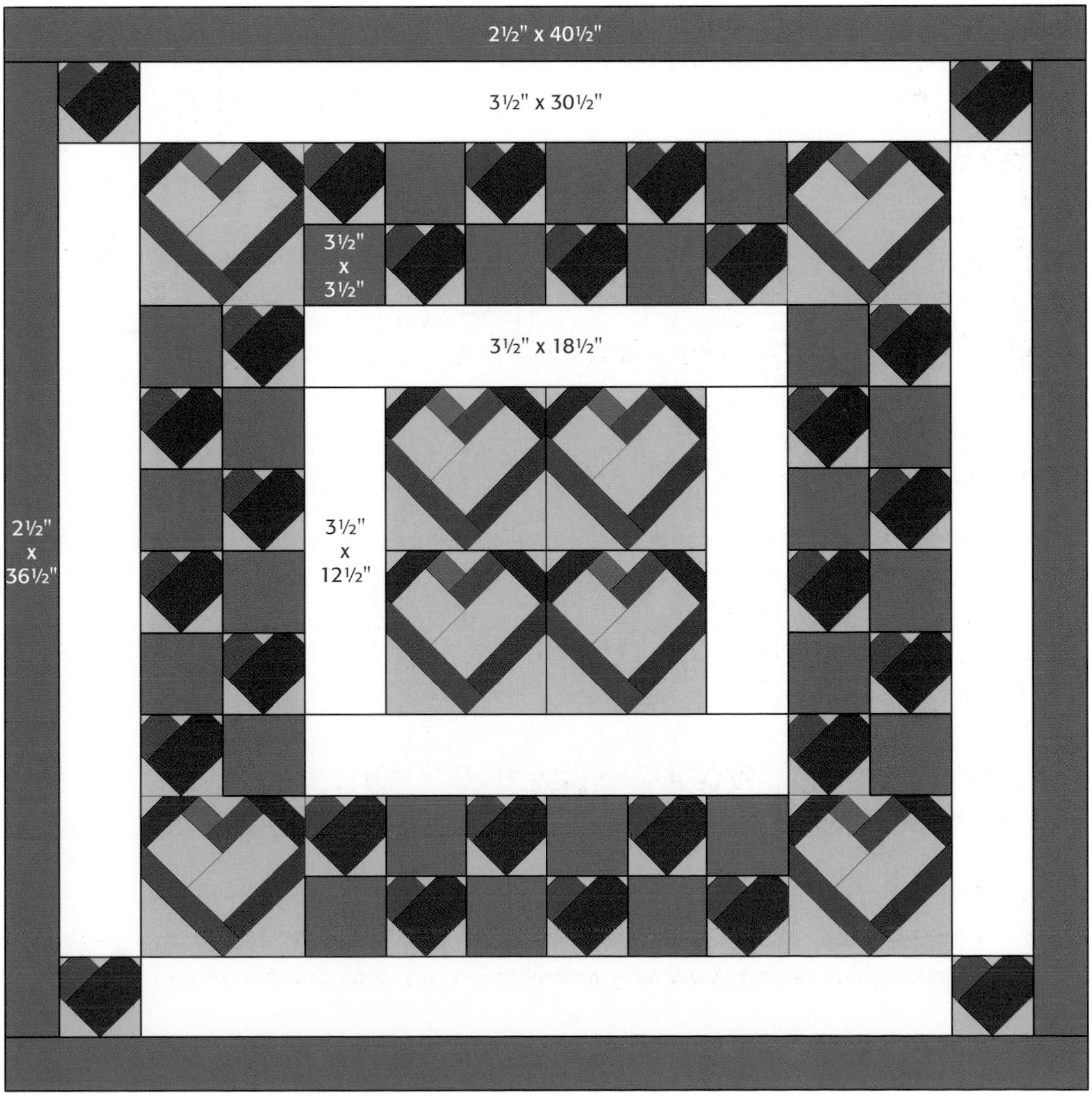

Measurements in quilt plan are cut sizes.

Cutting for Blocks

Fabric	No. of Pieces	Dimensions	Location Numbers	Block
Fuchsia #1	8	1½" x 2"	2	H22
Fuchsia #2	8	1½" x 3½"	8	H22
Fuchsia #3	28	1¾" x 2½"	1	H23
	8	1½" x 6½"	9	H22
	8	1½" x 3"	3	H22
Fuchsia #4	8	1½" x 5"	7	H22
Fuchsia #5	28	2½" x 3½"	3	H23
	8	1½" x 3½"	6	H22
Pink	8	4¼" x 4¼" ⧅	10, 11	H22
	2	3¼" x 3¼" ⊠	1	H22
	28	2¾" x 2¾" ⧅	4, 5	H23
	8	2½" x 4½"	5	H22
	8	2½" x 3"	4	H22
	8	2¼" x 2¼" ⧅	12, 13	H22
	7	2¼" x 2¼" ⊠	2	H23
	28	1¾" x 1¾" ⧅	6, 7	H23

Make the following paper-pieced blocks.

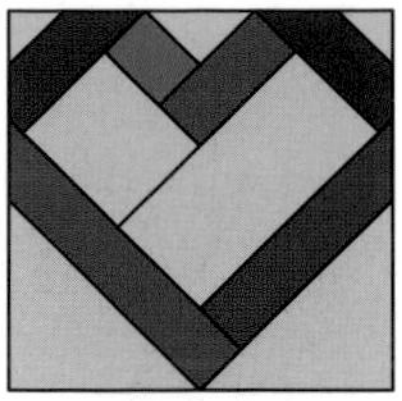

H22
Make 8
(page 78).

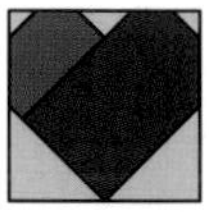

H23
Make 28
(page 78).

Tip

When assembling the quilt, remember to change the stitch length on the sewing machine to a regular stitch length when sewing across fabric, and to the small stitch when sewing across the paper foundations.

JUST DUCKY!

By Carol Doak, 2000, Windham, New Hampshire, 36½" x 36½". I had great fun making this quilt, which would be appropriate for either a little boy or a little girl! The radiating geometric design in the center was inspired by the fluffy duck tails. Machine quilted by Ellen Peters.

MATERIALS

42"-wide fabric

- 1⅜ yds. light blue for borders, binding, and blocks (nondirectional)
- ¼ yd. dark blue #1 for corner squares
- ¼ yd. dark blue #2 (nondirectional)
- ⅝ yd. yellow #1 (nondirectional)
- ¼ yd. yellow #2
- ¼ yd. yellow #3
- ¼ yd. yellow #4
- 1⅛ yds. for backing
- 40" x 40" piece of batting

CUTTING FOR BORDERS, BINDING, AND SETTING PIECES

Fabric	No. of Pieces	Dimensions	Location
Light blue	4	3½" x 30½"	Outer border
	4	3½" x 12½"	Inner border
	4	2" x 40"	Binding
Dark blue #1	16	3½" x 3½"	Corner squares

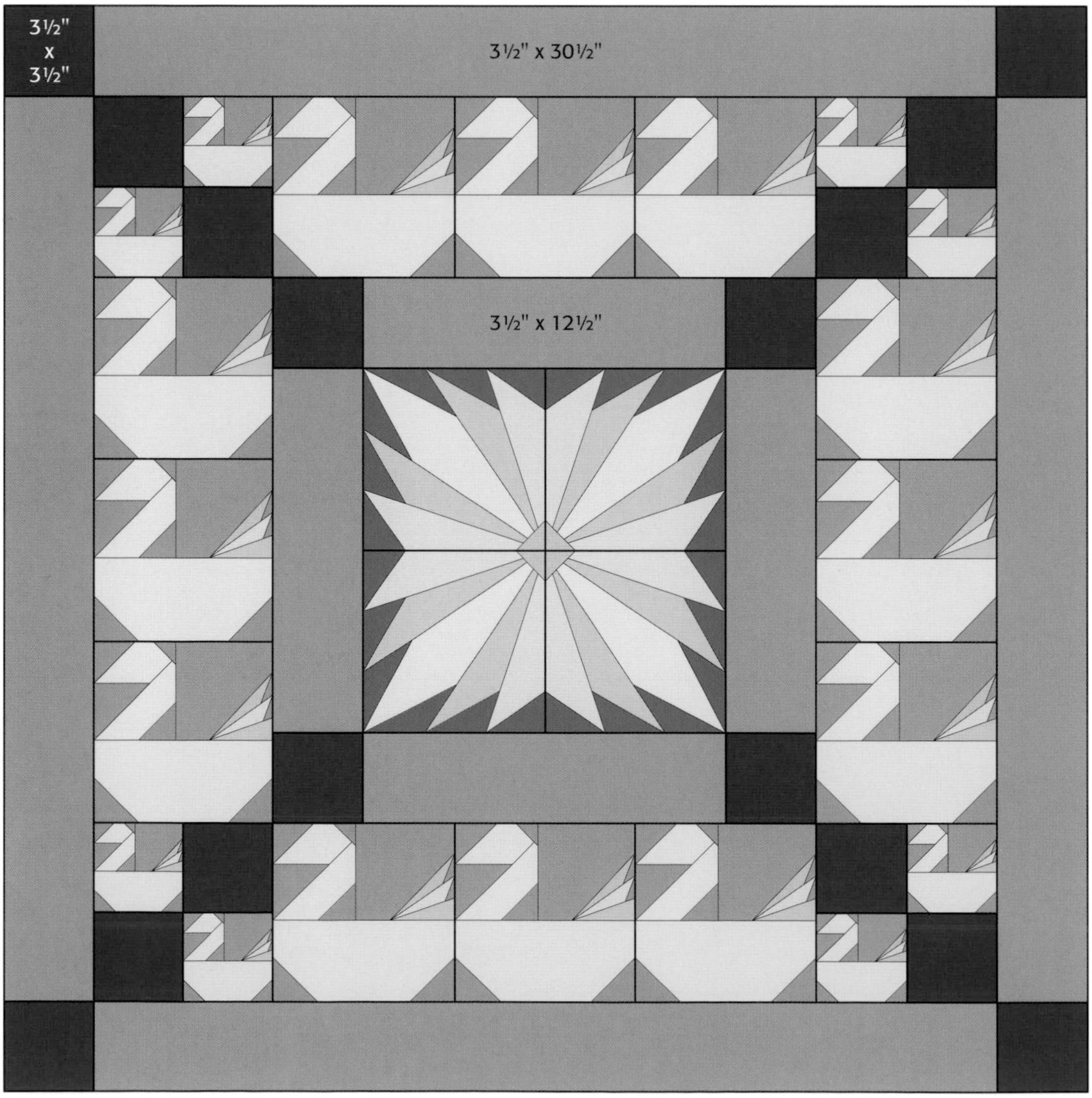

Measurements in quilt plan are cut sizes.

Cutting for Blocks

Fabric	No. of Pieces	Dimensions	Location Numbers	Block
Light blue	12	4" x 4"	7	P63 large
	6	3¼" x 3¼" ⧅	2	P63 large
	24	2¾" x 2¾" ⧅	4, 5, 14, 15	P63 large
	26	2¼" x 2¼" ⧅	2, 4, 5, 14, 15	P63 small
			6	P63 large
	8	2¼" x 2¼"	7	P63 small
	48	1" x 2"	9, 11	P63 large and small
			6	P63 small
Dark blue #2	24	1¾" x 4¼"	2, 3, 6, 7, 10, 11	G91
Yellow #1	12	3½" x 7"	13	P63 large
	4	3" x 9"	1	G91
	20	2" x 3¾"	1	P63 large
			13	P63 small
	12	1¾" x 4½"	3	P63 large
	16	1¼" x 2½"	1, 3	P63 small
Yellow #2	8	2" x 7½"	4, 5	G91
	12	1¼" x 3"	12	P63 large
	8	1" x 2"	12	P63 small
Yellow #3	8	2" x 6½"	8, 9	G91
	12	1¼" x 3½"	10	P63 large
	8	1" x 2"	10	P63 small
Yellow #4	12	1" x 4"	8	P63 large
	8	1" x 2¼"	8	P63 small
	2	2¼" x 2¼" ⧅	12	G91

Make the following paper-pieced blocks.

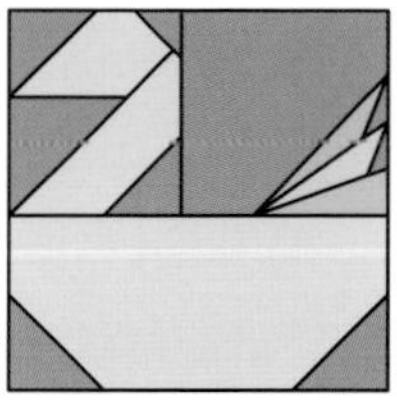

P63
Make 12 large
(page 79).

P63
Make 8 small
(page 79).

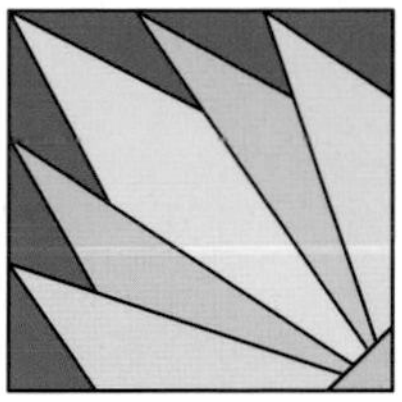

G91
Make 4
(page 80).

Tip

Trim the seam allowances to ⅛" rather than ¼" when paper piecing the tail feathers of the small duck.

PINWHEELS

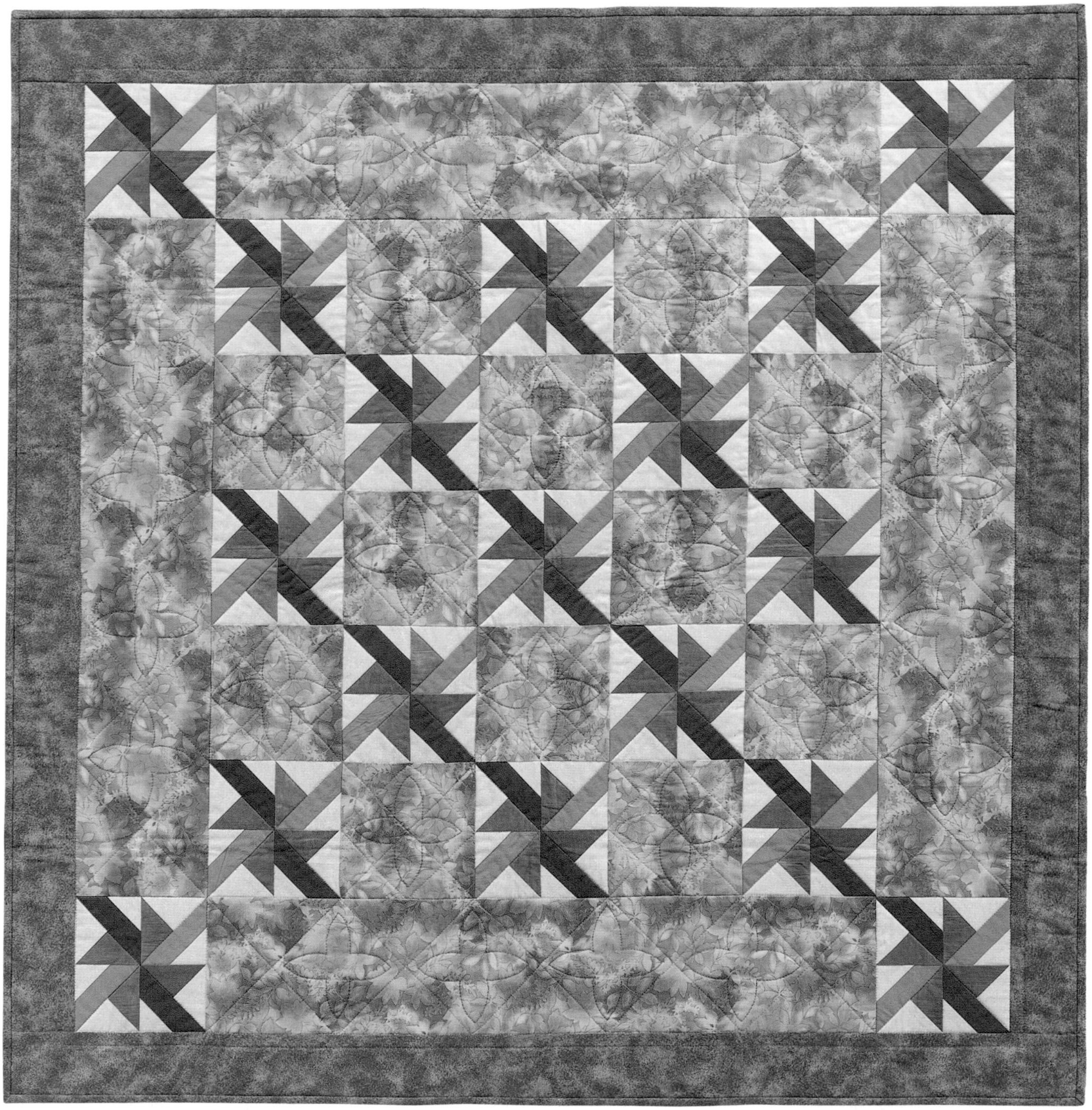

By Carol Doak, 2000, Windham, New Hampshire, 40½" x 40½". The multicolor border fabric was the inspiration for combining the solid colors used in the alternating pinwheel blocks. This is a happy quilt for either a little boy or a little girl. Machine quilted by Ellen Peters.

Materials

42"-wide fabric

- ¾ yd. green #1 for outer border and binding
- 1 yd. pastel print for inner border and alternating blocks
- ½ yd. white
- ¼ yd. pink
- ¼ yd. blue
- ¼ yd. green #2
- ¼ yd. purple
- 1¼ yds. for backing
- 44" x 44" piece of batting

Cutting for Borders, Binding, and Setting Pieces

Fabric	No. of Pieces	Dimensions	Location
Green #1	2	3" x 40½"	Outer top and bottom border
	2	3" x 35½"	Outer side border
	5	2" x 40"	Binding
Pastel print	4	5½" x 25½"	Inner border
	12	5½" x 5½"	Setting squares

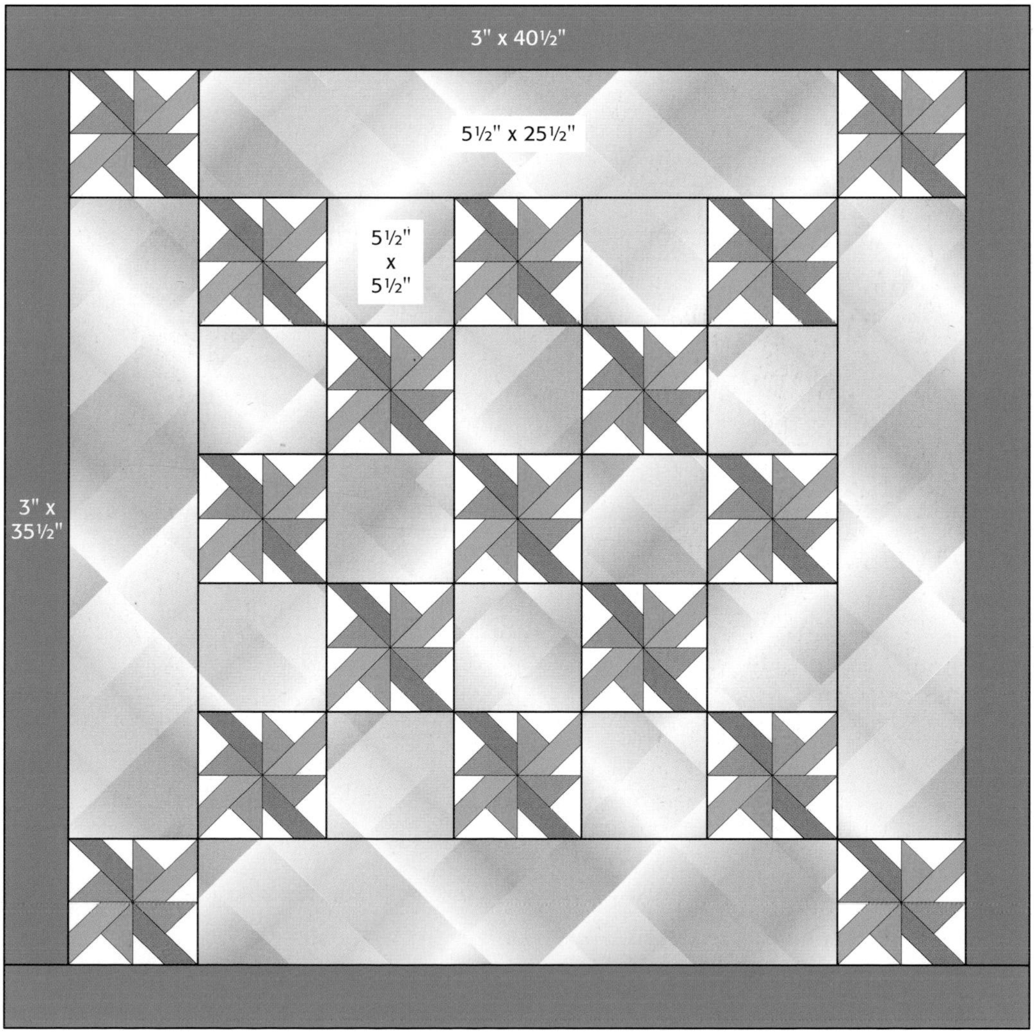

Measurements in quilt plan are cut sizes.

CUTTING FOR BLOCKS

Fabric	No. of Pieces	Dimensions	Location Numbers	Block
White	17	4" x 4" ⊠	2, 6	G92A, G92B
	34	2½" x 2½" ⧅	4, 8	G92A, G92B
Pink	9	4" x 4" ⊠	1	G92A, G92B
Blue	9	4" x 4" ⊠	5	G92A, G92B
Green #2	34	1½" x 4½"	3	G92A, G92B
Purple	34	1½" x 4½"	7	G92A, G92B

Make the following paper-pieced blocks.

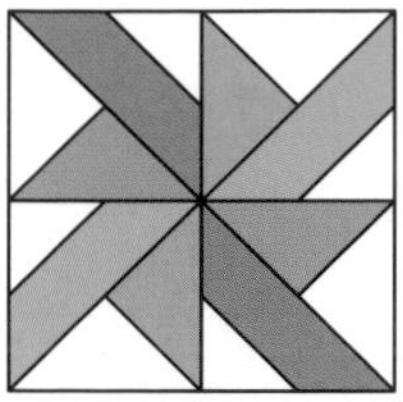

G92
Make 17
(page 81).

TIPS

- With just one block design, this is a really easy little quilt to make.
- Because there are so many seams coming together in the center of the block design, press the middle seam allowance open using a pressing cloth. Caution: do not place the iron directly to the back of the block, as the heat will smear the ink and cause some to transfer to the iron.

Baby Blocks

By Carol Doak, 2000, Windham, New Hampshire, 38½" x 38½". I have always loved the look of the traditional baby block quilts, but I have not been particularly anxious to sew all those angles. These paper-pieced baby blocks set in a square were my answer. Of course, having quilt patterns on the blocks made them just that much more fun to make. Machine quilted by Ellen Peters.

Materials

42"-wide fabric

- 1 yd. dark blue print for outer border and binding
- 1 yd. yellow for inner border, setting pieces, and blocks (nondirectional)
- ⅜ yd. medium green for blocks and inner corner squares (nondirectional)
- ⅜ yd. dark pink for middle corner squares and blocks (nondirectional)
- ¼ yd. medium pink (nondirectional)
- ⅜ yd. dark blue (nondirectional)
- ¼ yd. medium blue (nondirectional)
- ¼ yd. light green (nondirectional)
- 1¼ yds. for backing
- 42" x 42" piece of batting

Cutting for Borders, Binding, and Setting Pieces

Fabric	No. of Pieces	Dimensions	Location
Dark blue print	2	4½" x 38½"	Outer top and bottom border
	2	4½" x 30½"	Outer side border
	5	2" x 40"	Binding
Yellow	4	3½" x 24½"	Inner border
	12	3½" x 6½"	Setting rectangles
Medium green	4	3½" x 3½"	Inner corner squares
Dark pink	4	3½" x 3½"	Middle corner squares

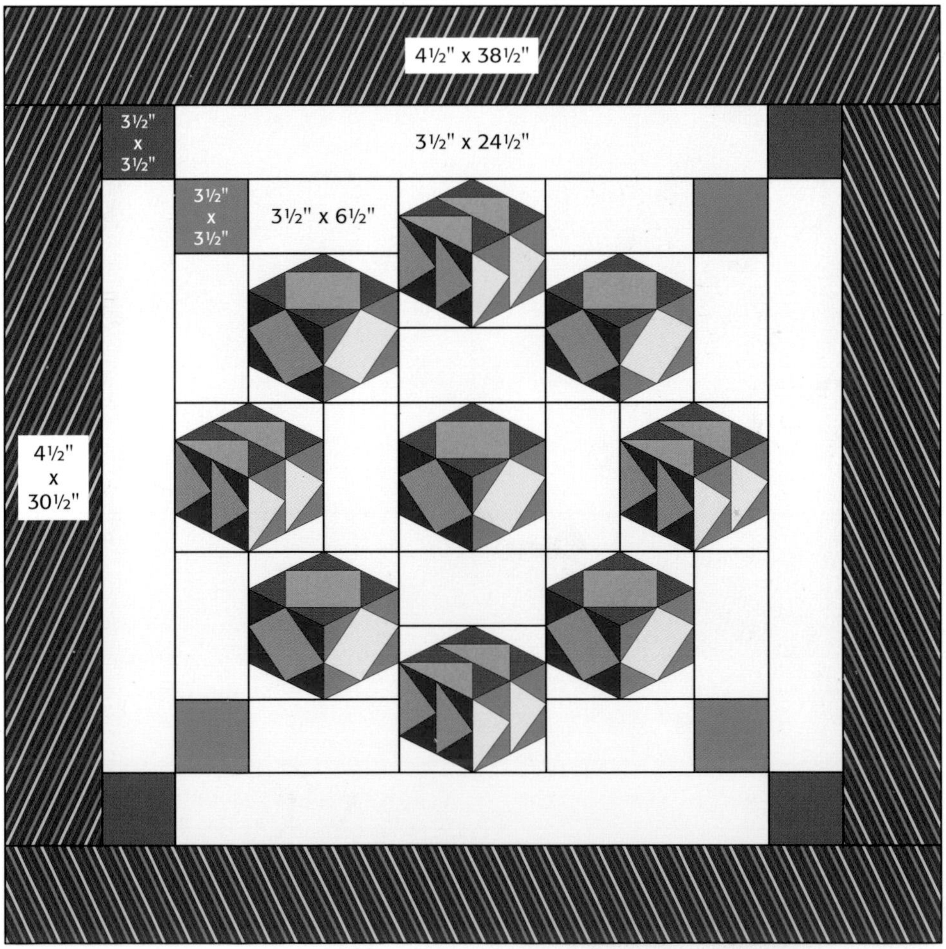

Measurements in quilt plan are cut sizes.

Cutting for Blocks

Fabric	No. of Pieces	Dimensions	Location Numbers	Block
Yellow	36	2" x 4½"	6, 7	P64C
			6	P64A, P64B
			7, 8	P65A
			13, 14	P65B
Dark pink	18	2¼" x 2¼"	4, 5	P64C
			3, 6	P65A
	18	1½" x 3¾"	2, 3	P64C
			2, 5	P65A
Medium pink	13	2¼" x 4"	1	P64C
			1, 4	P65A
Dark blue	18	2¼" x 2¼"	3, 5	P64B
			2, 5	P65B
	18	1½" x 4"	2, 4	P64B
			3, 6	P65B
Medium blue	13	2¼" x 4"	1	P64B
			1, 4	P65B
Medium green	18	2¼" x 2¼"	3, 5	P64A
			9, 12	P65B
	18	1½" x 4"	2, 4	P64A
			8, 11	P65B
Light green	13	2¼" x 4"	1	P64A
			7, 10	P65B

Make the following paper-pieced blocks.

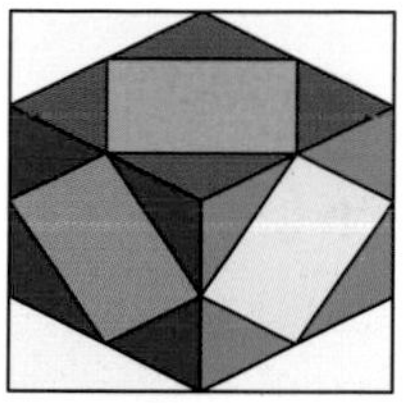

P64
Make 5
(page 82).

P65
Make 4
(page 83).

Tip

See page 18 before joining the sections of the baby blocks. It is not difficult, but the tips provided there will make it easier.

OLD MACDONALD'S FARM

By Carol Doak, 2000, Windham, New Hampshire, 46½" x 46½". This medallion-style quilt features a restful country scene. The barn in the center is surrounded by happy little ducks, flying geese, and green trees. Quilted flowers are blooming in the corner squares. This quilt has lots of detail and color that is sure to capture the attention of any little baby. Machine quilted by Ellen Peters.

Materials

42"-wide fabric

- 1¼ yds. medium green for outer border, binding, setting piece, and blocks (nondirectional)
- ¾ yd. medium blue for inner border and blocks (nondirectional)
- ⅜ yd. yellow for middle border and blocks (nondirectional)
- ½ yd. red for corner squares and blocks
- ½ yd. dark green (nondirectional)
- ½ yd. dark blue (nondirectional)
- 1⅛ yds. light blue (nondirectional)
- ¼ yd. black
- ⅛ yd. white
- 2¾ yds. for backing
- 48" x 48" piece of batting

Cutting for Borders, Binding, and Setting Pieces

Fabric	No. of Pieces	Dimensions	Location
Medium green	4	3½" x 40½"	Outer border
	5	2" x 40"	Binding
	1	3½" x 14½"	Barn setting piece
Medium blue	4	3½" x 14½"	Inner border
Yellow	2	1½" x 30½"	Middle top and bottom border
	2	1½" x 28½"	Middle side border
Red	4	5½" x 5½"	Corner squares
	4	4½" x 4½"	Corner squares
	4	3½" x 3½"	Corner squares

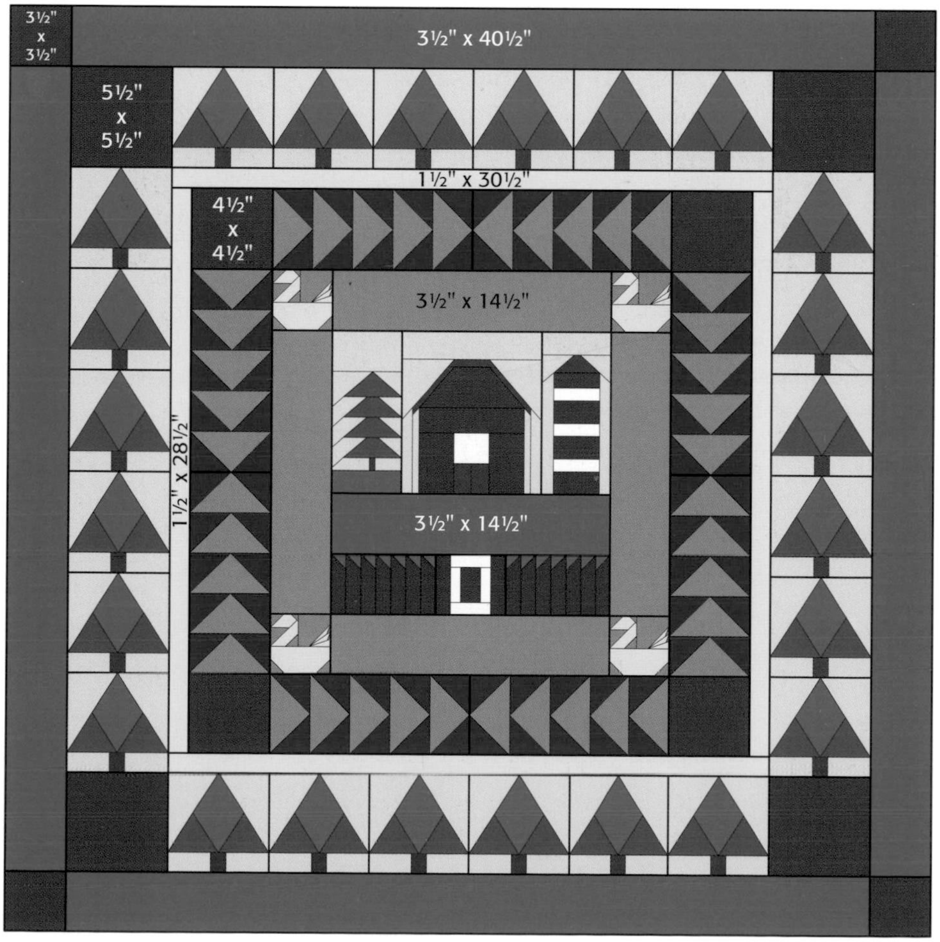

Measurements in quilt plan are cut sizes.

Cutting for Blocks

Fabric	No. of Pieces	Dimensions	Location Numbers	Block
Medium green	24	2¾" x 4½"	1	T22
	7	2" x 2" ⧄	even numbers	P68, P69
	1	1¾" x 4½"	4	T21
Dark green	48	2¾" x 3½"	2, 3	T22
	4	1¾" x 4¼"	5, 8, 11, 14	T21
Dark blue	40	3¼" x 3¼" ⧄	2, 3, 5, 6, 8, 9, 11	
			12, 14, 15	PB15
Medium blue	10	5½" x 5½" ⊠	1, 4, 7, 10, 13	PB15
	10	2¼" x 2¼" ⧄	2, 4, 5, 14, 15	P63
	4	2¼" x 2¼"	7	P63
	12	1" x 1"	6, 9, 11	P63
Light blue	1	4" x 4" ⧄	15, 16	P66
	5	3" x 3" ⧄	6, 7, 9, 10, 12, 13	
			15, 16	T21
			11, 12	P67
	2	2¾" x 42"	6 pieced unit	T22
	49	2¾" x 6"	4, 5	T22
			17	T21
	1	2" x 7¾"	17	P66
	1	1¾" x 4¼"	13	P67
	4	1¼" x 5"	7, 8, 13, 14	P66
	2	1¼" x 2½"	2, 3	T21
	2	1¼" x 6½"	9, 10	P67
Yellow	4	2" x 3¾"	13	P63
	20	1¼" x 2½"	1, 3, 8, 10, 12	P63
Red	2	3" x 6"	6, 9	P66
	2	2½" x 3¾"	4, 5	P66
	4	1¾" x 3"	1, 3, 5, 7	P67
	17	1½" x 3¾"	odd numbers	P68, P69
			1, 6, 7	P70
Black	1	1¼" x 42"	6 pieced unit	T22
	4	1½" x 3"	8	P67
			1, 2, 12	P66
	2	1" x 4½"	10, 11	P66
	1	1" x 1¼"	1	T21
White	1	2½" x 2½"	3	P66
	7	1¼" x 3"	2, 4, 6	P67
			2, 3, 4, 5	P70

Make the following paper-pieced blocks and borders.

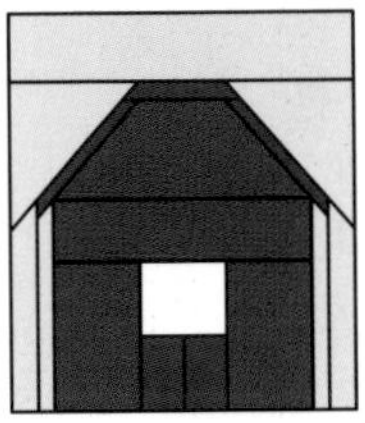
P66
Make 1
(page 84).

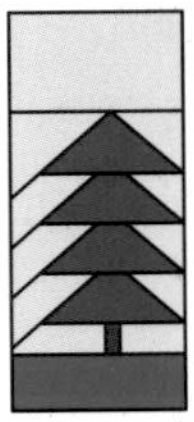
T21
Make 1
(page 85).

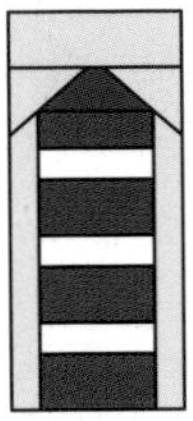
P67
Make 1
(page 86).

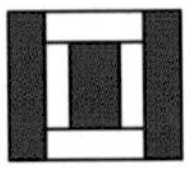
P70
Make 1
(page 88).

P63
Make 4 small
(page 79).

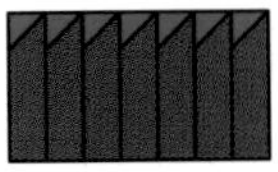
P68
Make 1
(page 87).

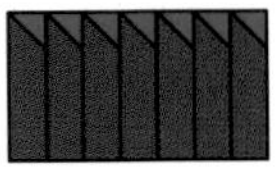
P69
Make 1
(page 87).

PB15
Make 8
(page 89).

T22
Make 24
(page 88).

Tips

- See page 16 to make the 24 pieced units #6 for T22.
- Trim the seam allowances to ⅛" rather than ¼" when paper piecing the tail feathers of the small duck.

SUGAR & SPICE

By Carol Doak, 2000, Windham, New Hampshire, 30½" x 36½". This quilt combines the themes of love and little girls. I used the same fabrics for each of my girls, but you could also make individual variations using different fabrics for each little girl. Machine quilted by Ellen Peters.

Materials

42"-wide fabric

- ¾ yd. medium pink for border, binding, and blocks
- ⅜ yd. dark pink (nondirectional)
- ⅞ yd. light pink (nondirectional)
- ¼ yd. pink calico (nondirectional)
- ⅛ yd. dark green
- ¼ yd. medium green
- ⅜ yd. light green
- ⅛ yd. cream
- 1⅛ yds. for backing
- 34" x 40" piece of batting

Cutting for Borders and Binding

Fabric	No. of Pieces	Dimensions	Location
Medium pink	4	3½" x 30½"	Border
	4	2" x 40"	Binding

Measurements in quilt plan are cut sizes.

CUTTING FOR BLOCKS

Fabric	No. of Pieces	Dimensions	Location Numbers	Block
Medium pink	10	1½" x 3"	5	P71A
Dark pink	10	1½" x 6½"	9	H22
	10	1½" x 5"	7	H22
	30	1½" x 3½"	3, 6, 8	H22
	10	1½" x 1¾"	2	H22
Light pink	10	4¼" x 4¼" ⧄	10, 11	H22
	3	3¼" x 3¼" ⊠	1	H22
	10	2½" x 4½"	5	H22
	10	2½" x 3½"	8	P71A
	20	2½" x 3"	9	P71B
			4	H22
	20	2¼" x 2¼" ⧄	12, 13	H22
			6, 7	P71B
	15	2" x 2" ⧄	1, 4, 5	P71B
	10	1¾" x 4¾"	12	P71A
	20	1½" x 3"	8, 12	P71B
	10	1½" x 2"	11	P71A
Pink calico	10	2" x 2¾"	3	P71B
	10	1½" x 2"	2	P71B
Dark green	10	1½" x 3¾"	10	P71A
	10	1¼" x 2½"	13	P71B
Medium green	10	2" x 5¾"	9	P71A
Light green	20	2¼" x 4½"	6, 7	P71A
	10	1¾" x 1¾"	4	P71A
	10	1¾" x 1¾" ⧄	2, 3	P71A
Cream	10	1½" x 3"	11	P71B
	10	1" x 3"	10	P71B
	10	1" x 1½"	1	P71A

Make the following paper-pieced blocks.

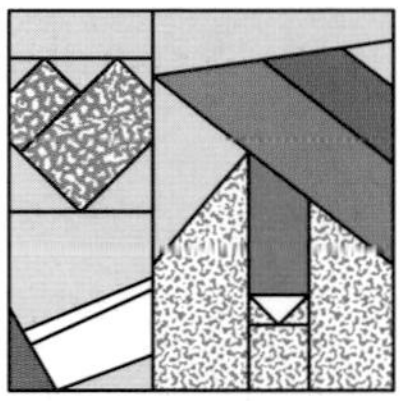

P71
Make 10
(page 90).

H22
Make 10
(page 78).

TIP

Use the machine-basting technique on page 17 when joining the blocks, to ensure that the center point of the heart block is accurately crossed.

Little Boy Love

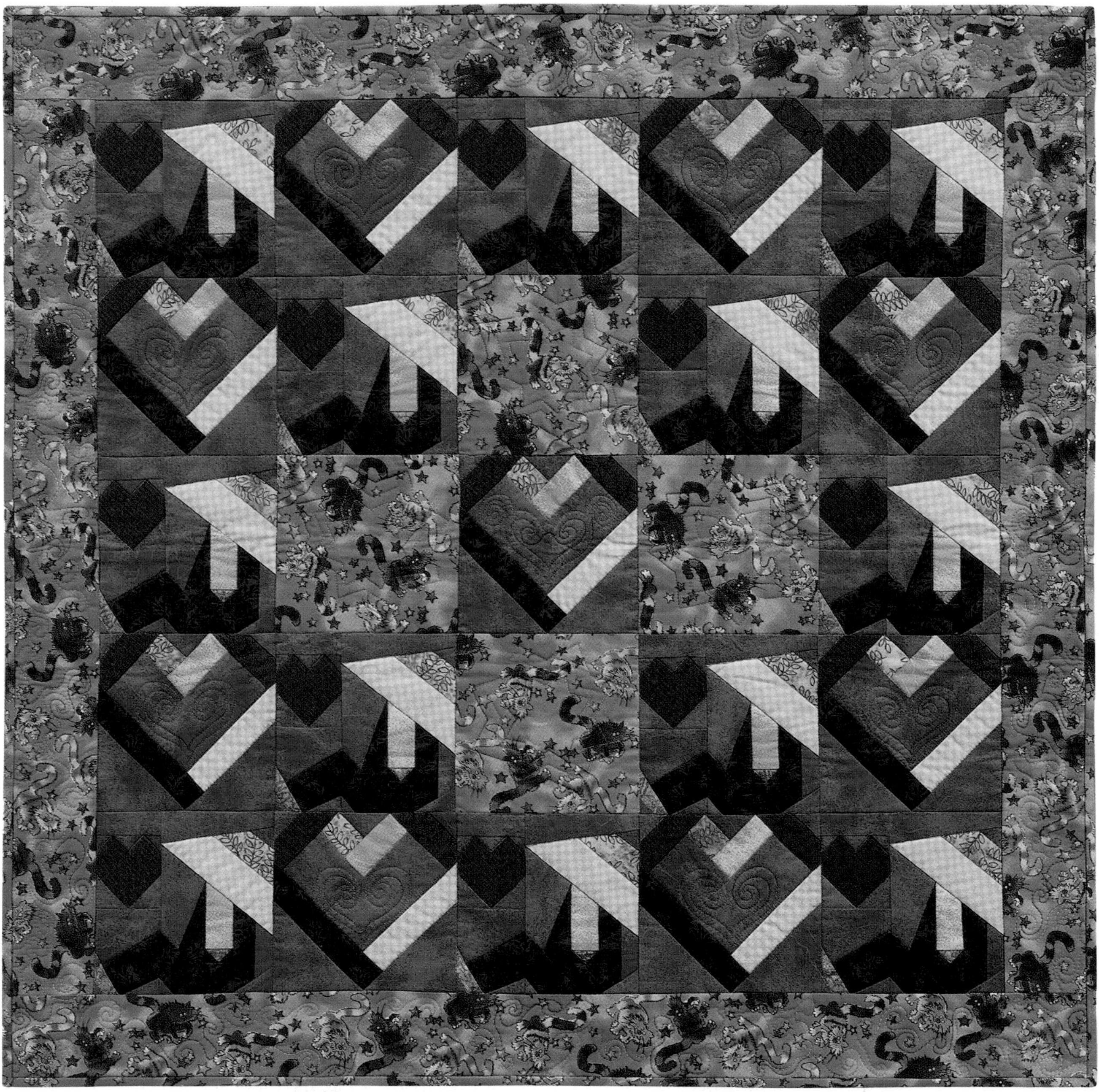

By Carol Doak, 2000, Windham, New Hampshire, 36½" x 36½". This brightly colored quilt combines a fun cat fabric for the border and center blocks with the little boy block and the heart block. The bright colors in the cat fabric were the inspiration for the colors in the pieced blocks. Machine quilted by Ellen Peters.

MATERIALS

42"-wide fabric

- 1 yd. novelty print for border, binding, and setting pieces
- ⅛ yd. light green
- 1 yd. medium blue (nondirectional)
- ½ yd. dark blue (nondirectional)
- ¼ yd. red
- ⅜ yd. yellow-and-white check
- ¼ yd. orange
- ⅛ yd. gold
- ⅛ yd. purple
- 1¼ yds. for backing
- 40" x 40" piece of batting

CUTTING FOR BORDERS, BINDING, AND SETTING PIECES

Fabric	No. of Pieces	Dimensions	Location
Novelty print	2	3½" x 36½"	Top and bottom border
	2	3½" x 30½"	Side border
	4	2" x 40"	Binding
	4	6½" x 6½"	Setting squares

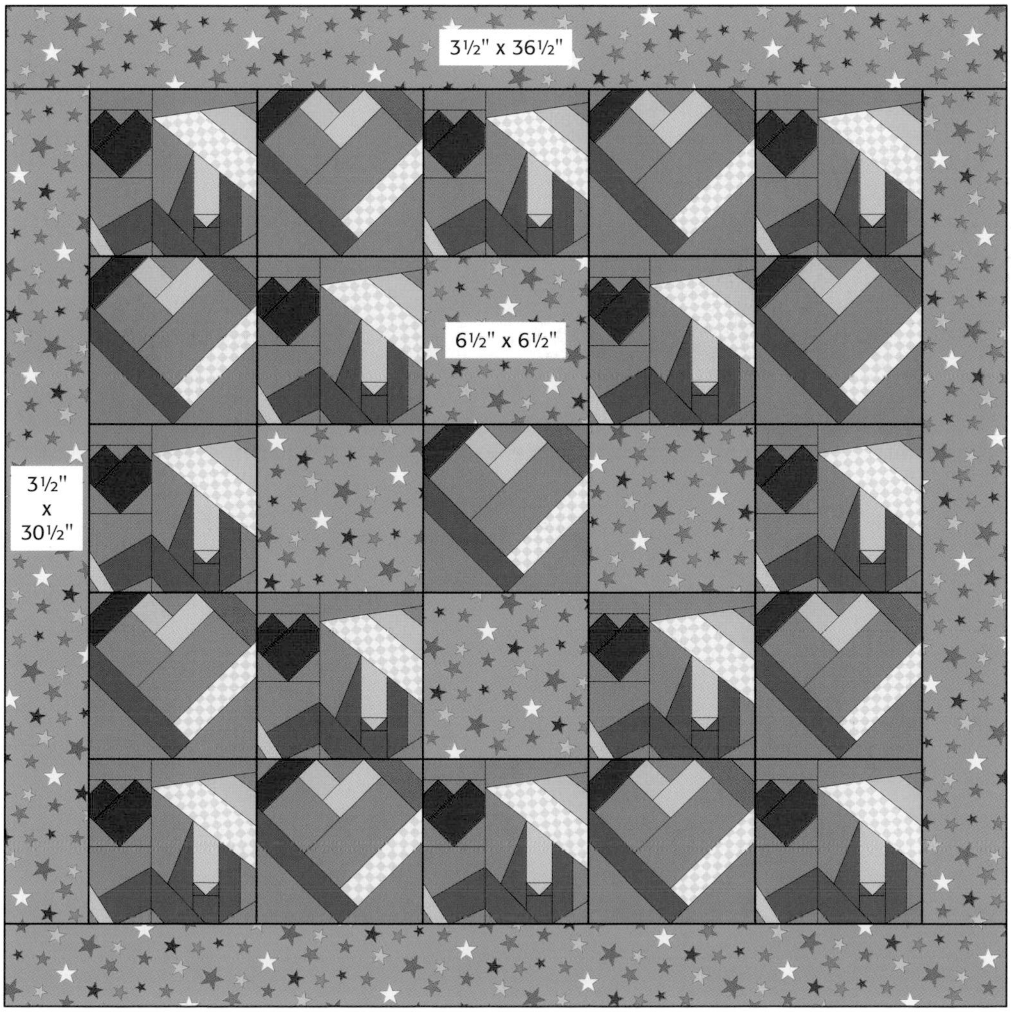

Measurements in quilt plan are cut sizes.

CUTTING FOR BLOCKS

Fabric	No. of Pieces	Dimensions	Location Numbers	Block
Light green	21	1½" x 3"	3	H22
			4	P72A
Medium blue	9	4¼" x 4¼" ⧅	10, 11	H22
	21	2½" x 4½"	5	H22
			8	P72A
	21	2½" x 3"	4	H22
			8	P72B
	18	2¼" x 2¼" ⧅	6, 7, 12	P72B
	45	2" x 2" ⧅	12, 13	H22
			1, 4, 5, 11	P72B
			11, 15	P72A
	12	1¾" x 4¾"	16	P72A
	12	1½" x 3"	13	P72B
	24	1½" x 2¾"	9, 12	P72A
	9	1½" x 2½"	1	H22
Dark blue	48	1¾" x 4"	6, 7, 10	P72A
			9	P72B
	12	1¾" x 1¾"	5	P72A
	12	1¾" x 1¾" ⧅	2, 3	P72A
	9	1½" x 6½"	9	H22
Red	12	2" x 3"	3	P72B
	9	1½" x 3½"	8	H22
	12	1½" x 2"	2	P72B
Yellow/white check	12	2" x 6"	13	P72A
	9	1½" x 5½"	7	H22
Orange	12	1½" x 3½"	14	P72A
	9	1½" x 2"	2	H22
Gold	12	1¼" x 3"	10	P72B
	12	1" x 1½"	1	P72A
Purple	9	1½" x 4"	6	H22

Make the following paper-pieced blocks.

P72
Make 12
(page 91).

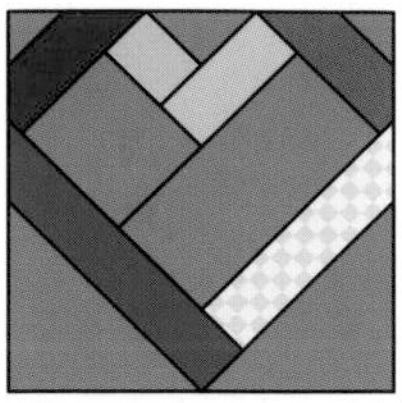

H22
Make 9
(page 78).

TIP

Use the machine-basting technique on page 17 when joining sections for P72, to align these sections properly.

The Night Train

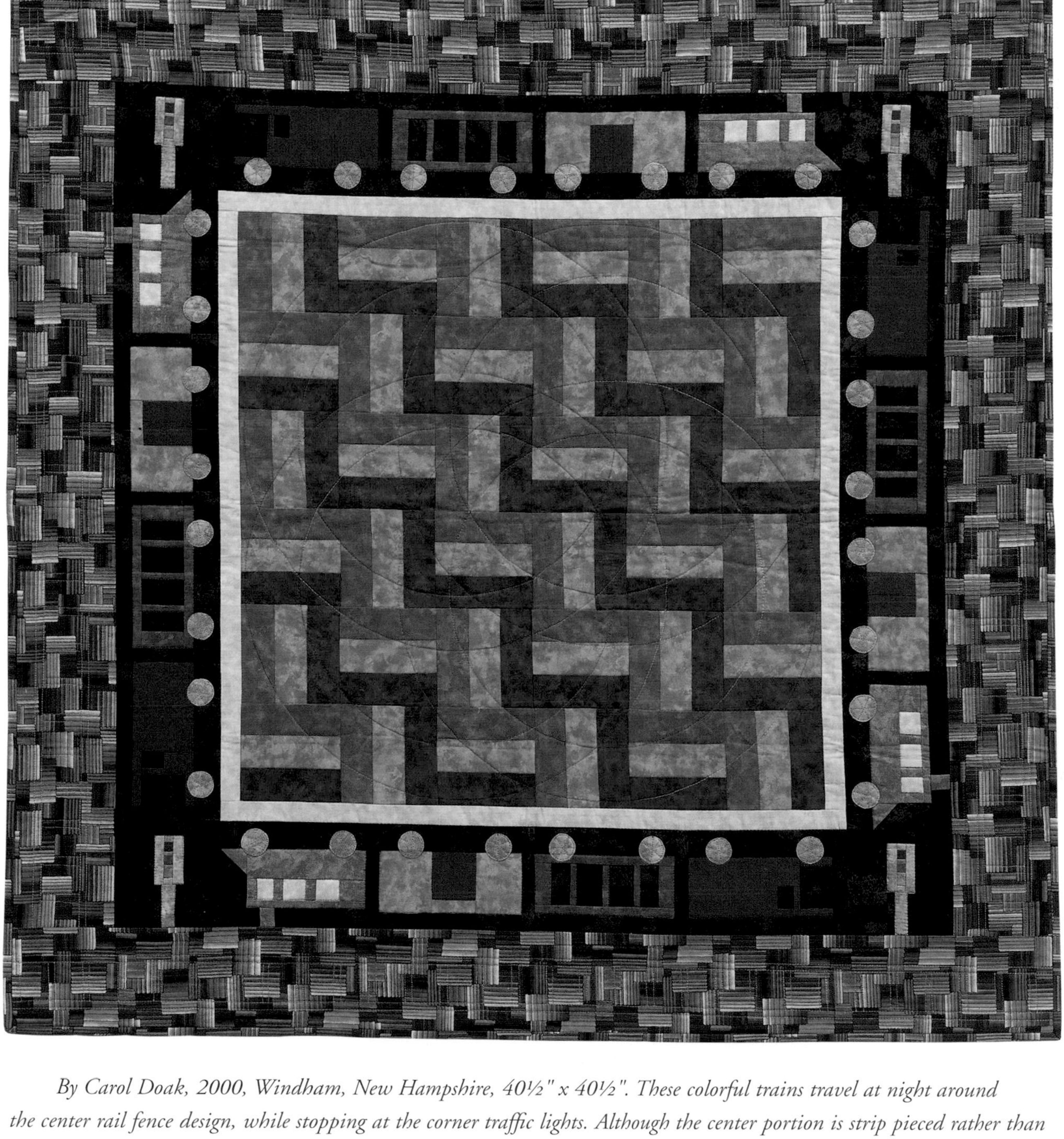

By Carol Doak, 2000, Windham, New Hampshire, 40½" x 40½". These colorful trains travel at night around the center rail fence design, while stopping at the corner traffic lights. Although the center portion is strip pieced rather than paper pieced, it was easily accomplished and provides the perfect setting for the paper-pieced train borders. The train wheels were applied using a fusible appliqué method. The large circular quilted wheels in the center portion of the quilt continue the theme. Machine quilted by Ellen Peters.

Materials

42"-wide fabric

- 1 yd. multicolor fabric for border and binding
- ¼ yd. light green for border and blocks
- ⅜ yd. orange*
- ⅜ yd. medium green*
- ¼ yd. medium blue**
- ⅝ yd. navy
- ¼ yd. light blue
- ¼ yd. red
- ¼ yd. gold
- 1¼ yds. for backing
- 44" x 44" piece of batting

* Use the traditional 13½" x 42"-wide yardage.
** Use the traditional 9" x 42"-wide yardage.

Cutting for Borders, Binding, and Center Patchwork

Fabric	No. of Pieces	Dimensions	Location
Multicolor	2	4½" x 40½"	Outer top and bottom border
	2	4½" x 32½"	Outer side border
	5	2" x 40"	Binding
Light green	2	1¼" x 24½"	Inner top and bottom border
	2	1¼" x 23"	Inner side border
Orange	4	1¾" x 42"	Strips for center patchwork
Medium green	4	1¾" x 42"	Strips for center patchwork
Medium blue	4	1¾" x 42	Strips for center patchwork

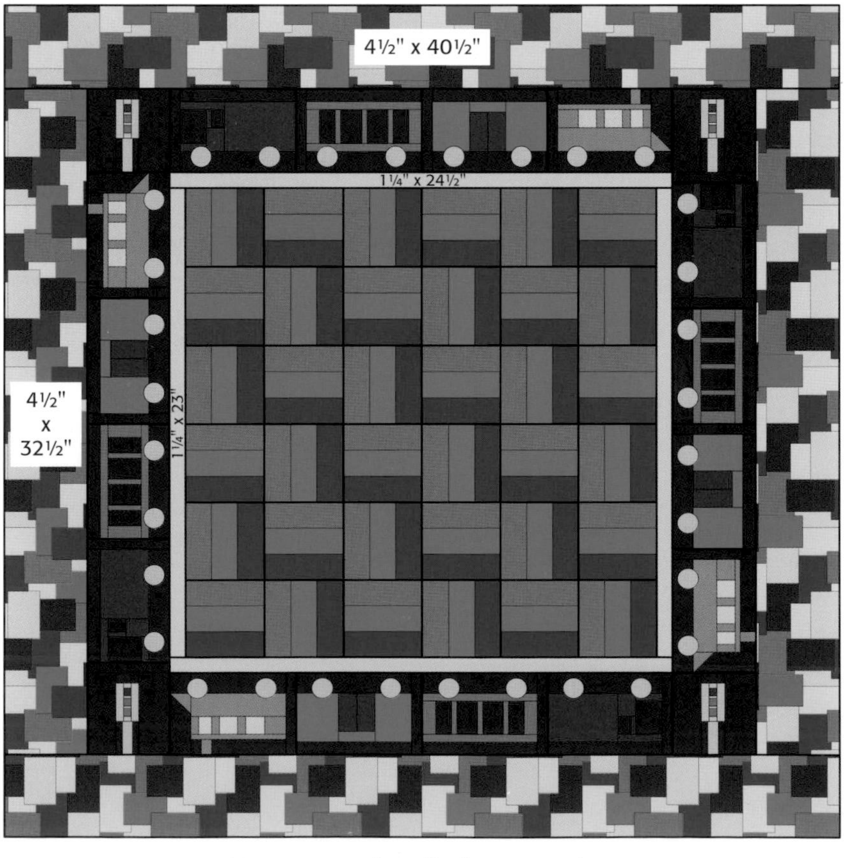

Measurements in quilt plan are cut sizes.

Cutting for Blocks

Fabric	No. of Pieces	Dimensions	Location Numbers	Block
Navy	8	2" x 4¾"	12, 13	P77
	4	2" x 2¼"	4*	P76
	24	1¾" x 6¼"	6, 7	P74
			12, 13	P75
			7, 8	P76
	12	1¾" x 5¼"	10, 11*, 12	P73B
	4	1¾" x 3¾"	1	P73A
	8	1¾" x 1¾"	3	P73A
			11*	P73B
	16	1½" x 2¼"	2, 4, 6, 8	P75
	4	1½" x 1½"	1	P76
	12	1¼" x 4¾"	8	P74
			14	P75
			9	P76
	4	1¼" x 2"	11	P77
	8	1" x 2½"	10*	P77
Light blue	2	2¼" x 2¼" ⧄	2	P73A
	4	1¾" x 5¼"	8	P73B
	4	1½" x 1½"	7	P73B
	4	1" x 5¼"	9	P73B
	12	1" x 1½"	1, 3, 5	P73B
	4	1" x 1¾"	11*	P73B
Red	4	3" x 4"	6	P76
	12	1½" x 2½"	1, 2	P74
			3	P76
	4	1" x 2¾"	5	P76
	8	1" x 2"	2, 4*	P76
	4	1" x 1"	2	P77
Orange	20	1¼" x 2¼"	1, 3, 5, 7, 9	P75
	8	1" x 6¼"	10, 11	P75
	4	1" x 1"	4	P77
Gold	12	1" x 2½"	8, 9, 10*	P77
	16	1" x 1"	1, 3, 5, 7	P77
Medium green	8	2¾" x 3"	4, 5	P74
	4	1¼" x 2½"	3	P74
	4	1" x 1"	6	P77
Light green	12	1½" x 1½"	2, 4, 6	P73B

* See Tips on page 58 for directions on making pieced units.

Make the following paper-pieced blocks.

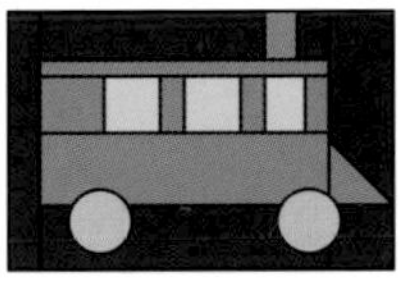

P73
Make 4
(page 92).

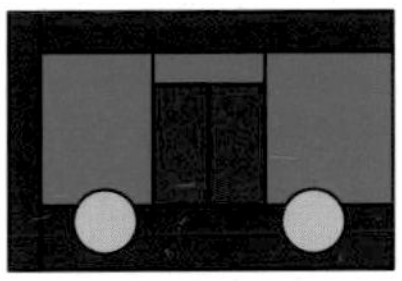

P74
Make 4
(page 92).

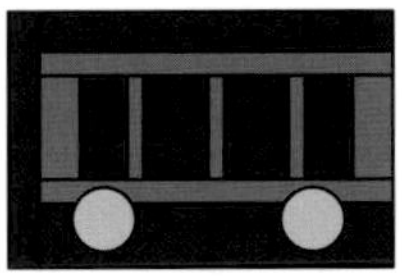

P75
Make 4
(page 93).

P76
Make 4
(page 93).

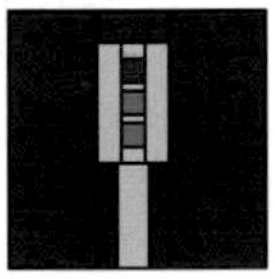

P77
Make 4
(page 94).

Center Patchwork Rail Fence Blocks

1. Sew a 1¾"-wide orange, green, and blue strip together to make each of 4 strip units. From each strip unit, cut 9 squares, 4¼" x 4¼", for a total of 36 squares.

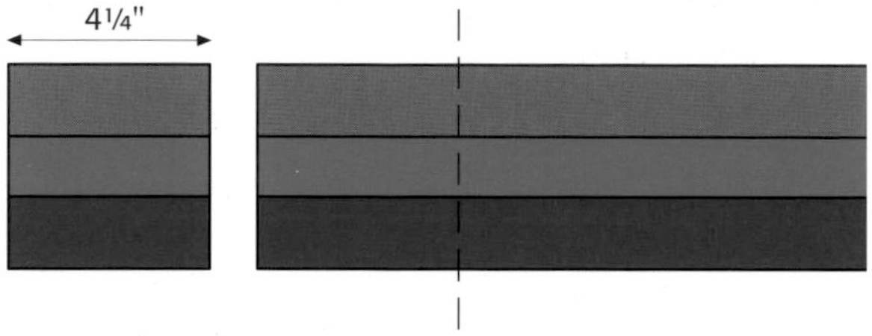

2. Arrange and sew the pieced squares in 6 rows of 6 blocks each, referring to the color photo on page 55. Press the seam allowances in opposite directions from row to row. Join the rows. The center section should measure 23" x 23".
3. Trace the circle on the foundation onto template material. Mark and cut 32 circles from the gold fabric for the wheels. I fused the circles to the train blocks and reinforced them with quilting stitches. You may use this method, machine appliqué them, or hand appliqué them. If you hand appliqué them, remember to add seam allowances to the templates. Use the foundations as your guide for placement.

TIPS

- Check the accuracy of your ¼" seam allowance before making the strip sets. If your seam allowance is not accurate, your center portion won't be accurate.
- To make the pieced units for #11 for P73B, join the pieces as shown. Make a total of 4 pieced units (see page 16 for information about pieced units).

Make 4.

- To make the pieced units for #4 for P76, join the pieces as shown. Make a total of 4 pieced units.

Make 4.

- To make the pieced units for #10 for P77, join the pieces as shown. Make a total of 4 pieced units.

Make 4.

QUILT FINISHING

CONGRATULATIONS! YOUR quilt top is now complete and ready to be sandwiched with the batting and backing of the quilt.

BASTING THE QUILT

THE QUILT sandwich consists of the backing, the batting, and the quilt top. There are many types of quilt batting available. I like to use a thin, low-loft polyester quilt batting when hand quilting, since it makes smaller stitches on small designs easier. When machine quilting, I prefer a cotton quilt batting, because the cotton fibers tend to grip the fabric.

1. Cut the backing and batting 2" to 3" larger than the quilt top all around. Remove the paper from the back of the quilt by tugging against the stitching.
2. Spread the backing, wrong side up, on a clean surface. Use masking tape or large binder clamps to anchor the backing to the table. Be careful not to stretch it out of shape.
3. Spread and smooth the quilt batting over the backing. Make sure it covers the entire backing.
4. Place the quilt top on top of the batting, right side up, smoothing out any wrinkles. Make sure the edges of the quilt top are parallel to the edges of the backing.
5. Beginning in the center and working to the outside edges, make diagonal, vertical and horizontal rows of basting stitches in a grid. If you plan to machine quilt, you may pin baste with size 2, rustproof safety pins.

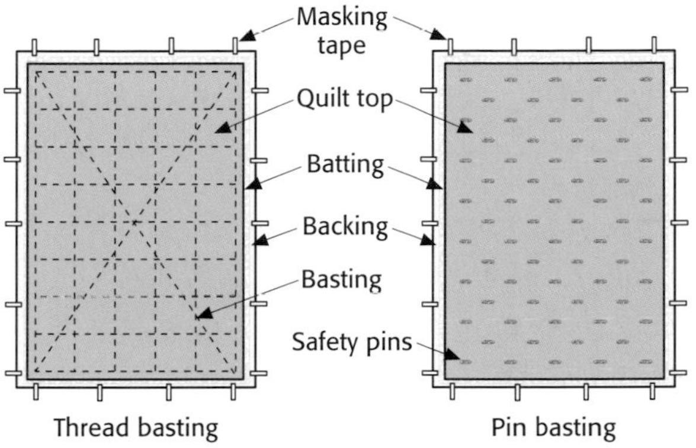

6. Bring the edge of the backing around to the front of the quilt top and baste in place in order to contain any exposed batting while quilting.

QUILTING THE QUILT

YOU MAY quilt your baby quilts by hand or by machine, or use a combination of both. If you prefer to hand quilt, keep in mind that the pieces in some of the smaller blocks don't leave a large amount of single layer fabric available for hand quilting, so plan your quilting designs accordingly. Use the larger open areas of the quilt to showcase your hand quilting designs. Rather than outline quilting the patches in the smaller patchwork areas, rely upon a single line of quilting.

If you are going to machine quilt, you can bring attention and detail to an area of the quilt by using a contrasting color thread. For example, the little flowers in the corner blocks of the "Old MacDonald's Farm" quilt (see page 46) really stand out and contribute to the detail in the quilt.

Adding a Sleeve

If you plan to hang the baby quilt, you will want to baste the raw edges of a sleeve to the quilt before adding the binding.

1. Cut a strip of fabric as long as the width of the quilt and double the desired depth of the sleeve plus ½" for seam allowances. Hem both ends of the strip.

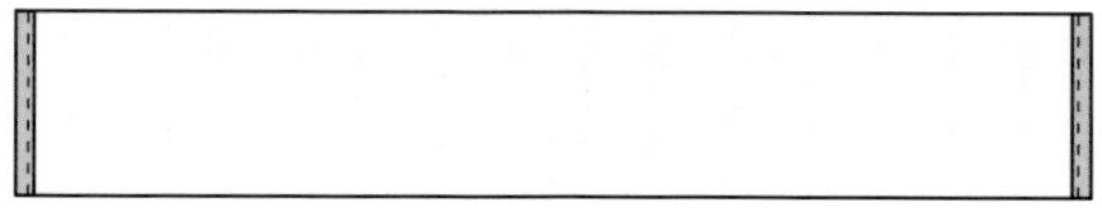

2. Fold the strip wrong sides together, and pin the raw edges at the top of the quilt before you attach the binding. Machine baste in place ⅛" from the edge. Add the binding to the quilt.

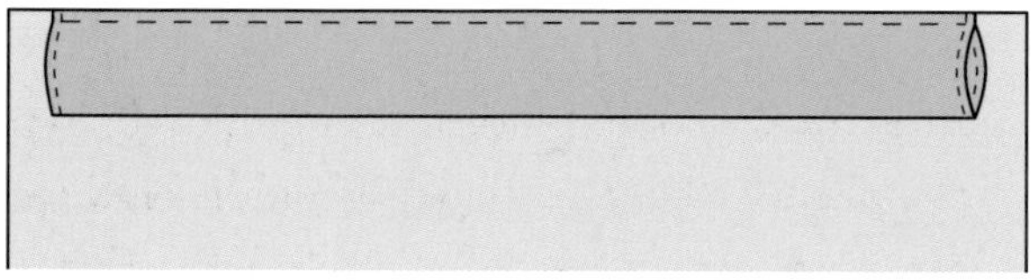

3. Blind stitch the folded edge of the sleeve to the back of the quilt.

Binding the Edges

Once you have completed the quilting, prepare the quilt for binding by removing the basting stitches (or safety pins) and trimming the batting and backing even with the edge of the quilt top. Adjust your machine for a basting-length stitch and use a walking foot or an even-feed foot, if available, to stitch around the perimeter of the quilt sandwich approximately ⅛" from the edge. The walking foot aids in sewing all three layers smoothly. If you are adding a sleeve to hang the baby quilt, baste it in place now (see above).

The directions for the baby quilts include information for cutting strips for straight-grain binding strips.

1. Join the ends of the strips at a 45° angle to make a strip long enough to go around the perimeter of the quilt, plus about 10".
2. Trim excess fabric, press seams open, and clip the "dog" ears.

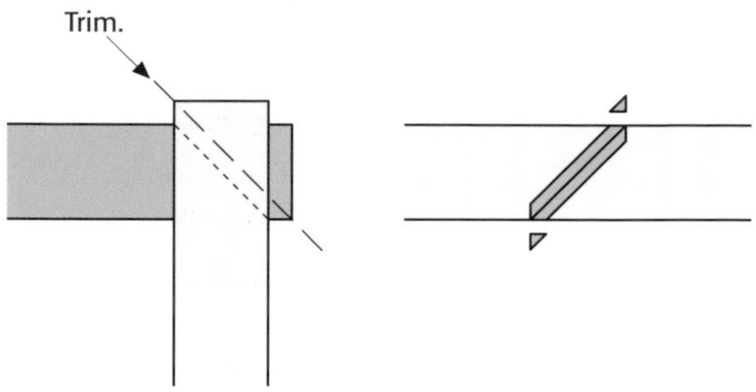
Trim.

To attach the binding:

1. Place the binding strip, wrong side up, on the cutting mat. Align a rotary ruler's 45°-angle marking with the edge of the strip near one end. Draw a "cutting line."

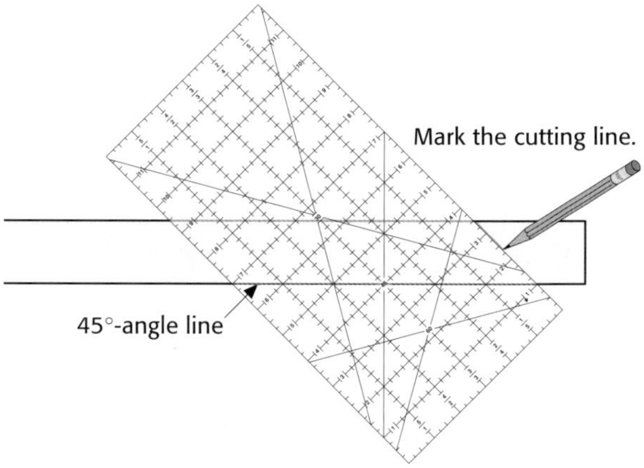
Mark the cutting line.
45°-angle line

Turn the strip and draw 2 more lines, each ¼" from the previous line.

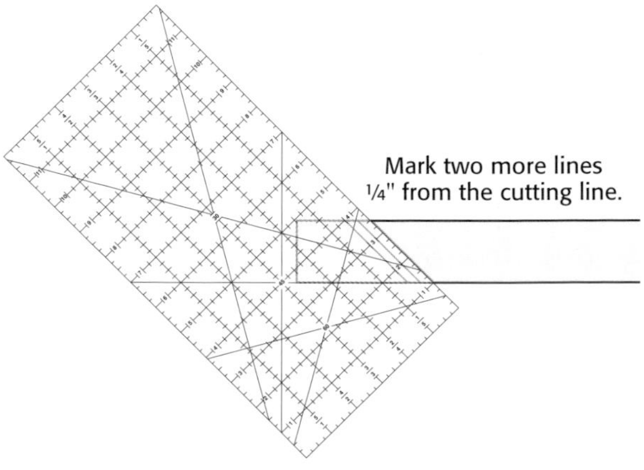
Mark two more lines
¼" from the cutting line.

The first line is the "cutting line," the second is the "sewing line," and the third is the "measuring line." Cut on the cutting line.

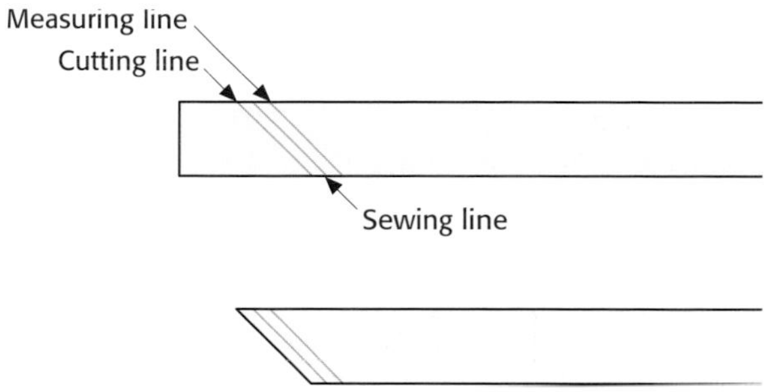

2. Fold the strip in half lengthwise, wrong sides together, and press.

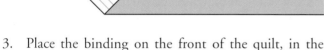

3. Place the binding on the front of the quilt, in the middle of the bottom edge, aligning the raw edges of the binding with the edge of the quilt. Attach a walking foot or even-feed foot to your sewing machine. Starting about 6" from the end of the binding, sew the binding to the quilt with a ¼"-wide seam allowance. Stop stitching ¼" from the corner of the quilt and backstitch.

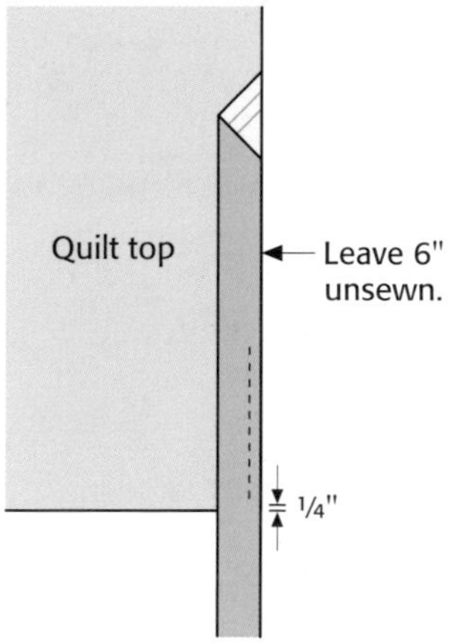

4. Turn the quilt to sew the next edge. Fold the binding up, away from the quilt, and then down, even with the next side. The straight fold should be even with the upper edge of the quilt. Stitch from the edge to the next corner, stopping ¼" from the corner. Repeat for the remaining corners.

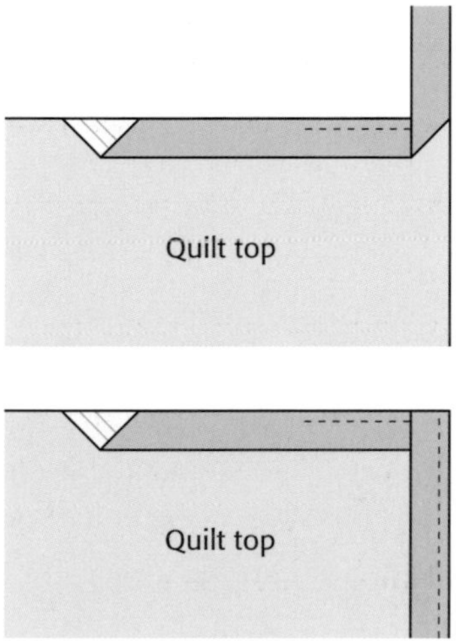

5. After the last corner is stitched, stop. Unfold the strip and place it under the beginning of the binding. On the wrong side, mark the raw edge of the strip at the measuring line on the beginning strip.

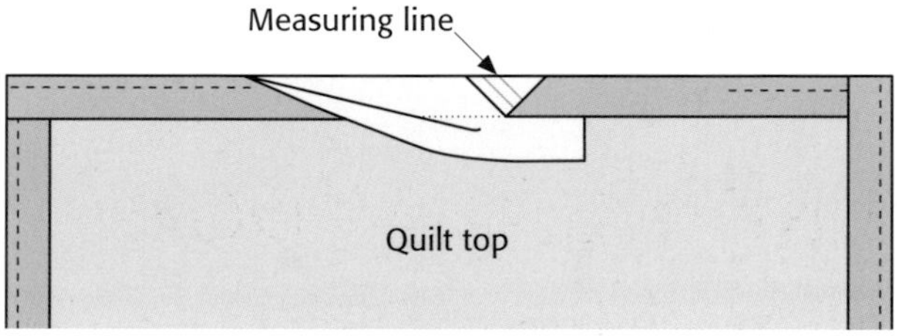

6. Align the rotary ruler's 45°-angle line with the straight edge of the end tail, with the edge of the ruler at the mark. Draw a cutting line. Draw a sewing line ¼" away as shown. **Place the binding strip on the cutting table, away from the quilt,** and cut on the cutting line.

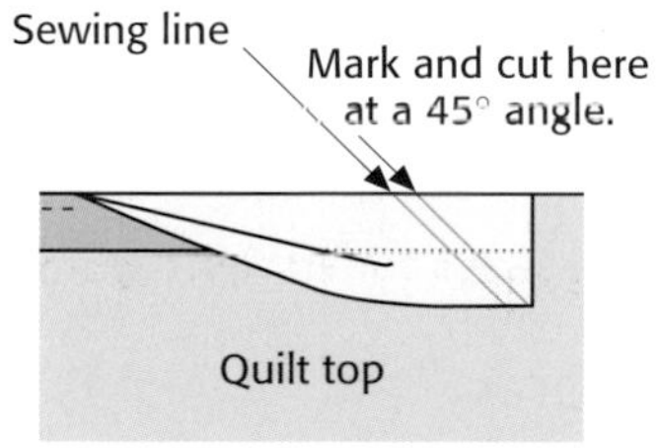

Wrong side of the binding strip

7. Pull the ends of the binding strips away from the quilt. Place the unfolded strips right sides together as shown. Pin, matching the 2 sewing lines, and stitch. Press the seam allowances open. Clip the "dog ears" and press the strip in half again.

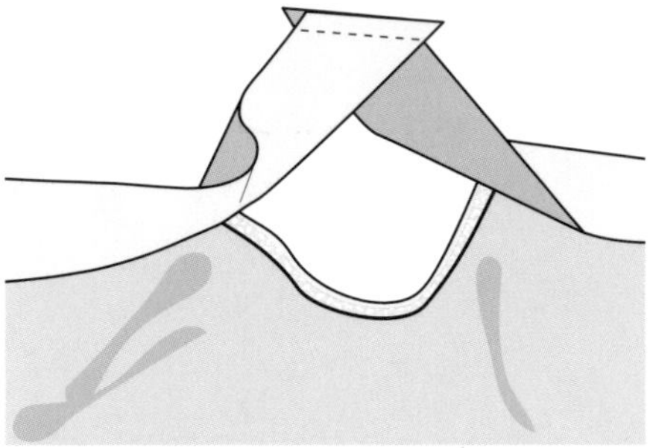

8. Return the strip to the edge of the quilt and finish the seam.

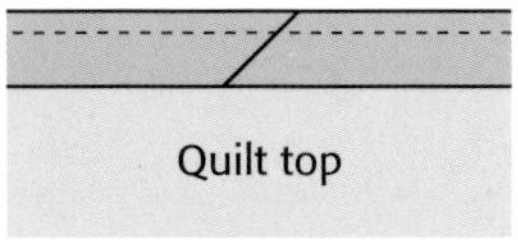

9. Fold the binding to the back, over the raw edges of the quilt. The folded edge of the binding should cover the machine stitching lines. Blind stitch in place.

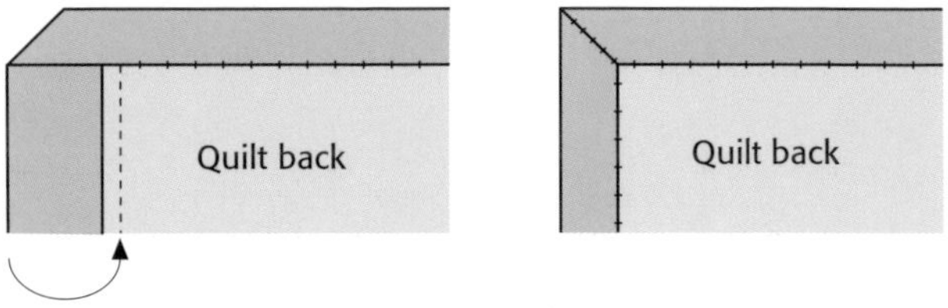

Signing Your Work

Your baby quilt is not finished until you add your label to the back of the quilt. This "signature" should contain your name, where and when the quilt was made, and the name of the special baby who will receive it. You can use a permanent marker or paint pen to write your information on a simple piece of fabric or on a special paper-pieced block that you make for this purpose. Be sure to choose fabric that will contrast well with your marker or pen.

Paper-Piecing Designs

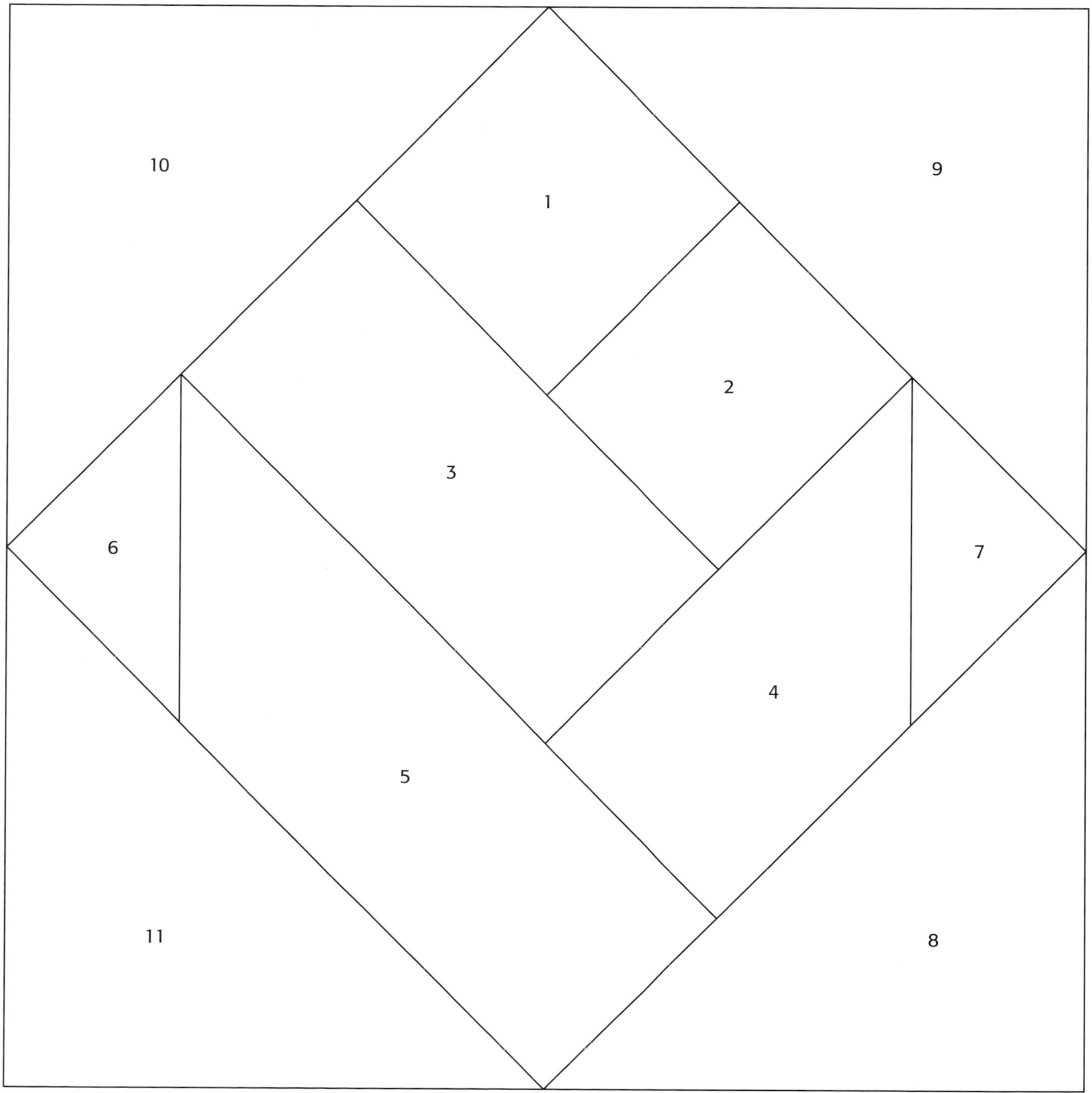

H19 (7" block)

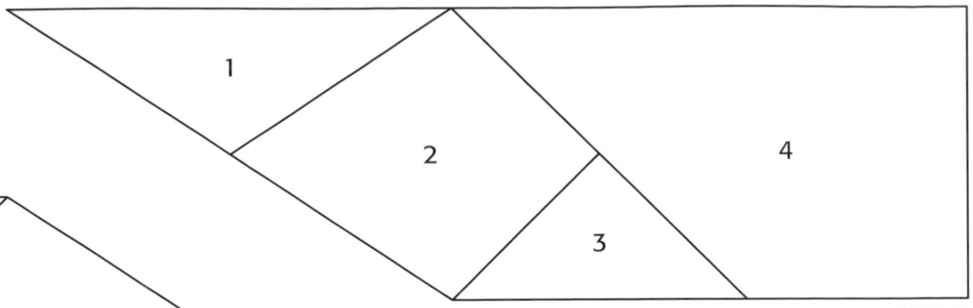

P56A

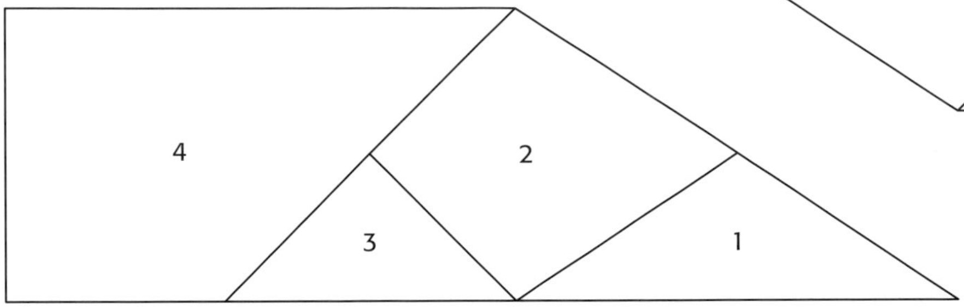

P56B

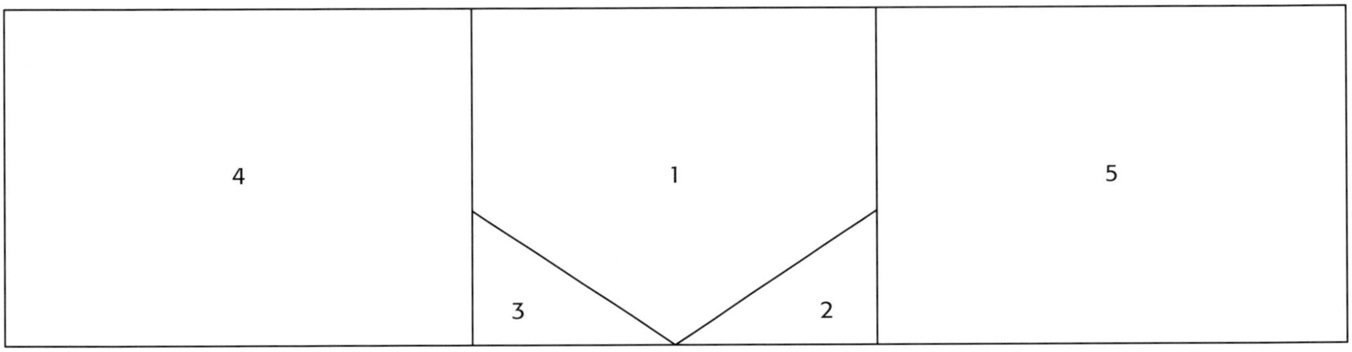

P56C

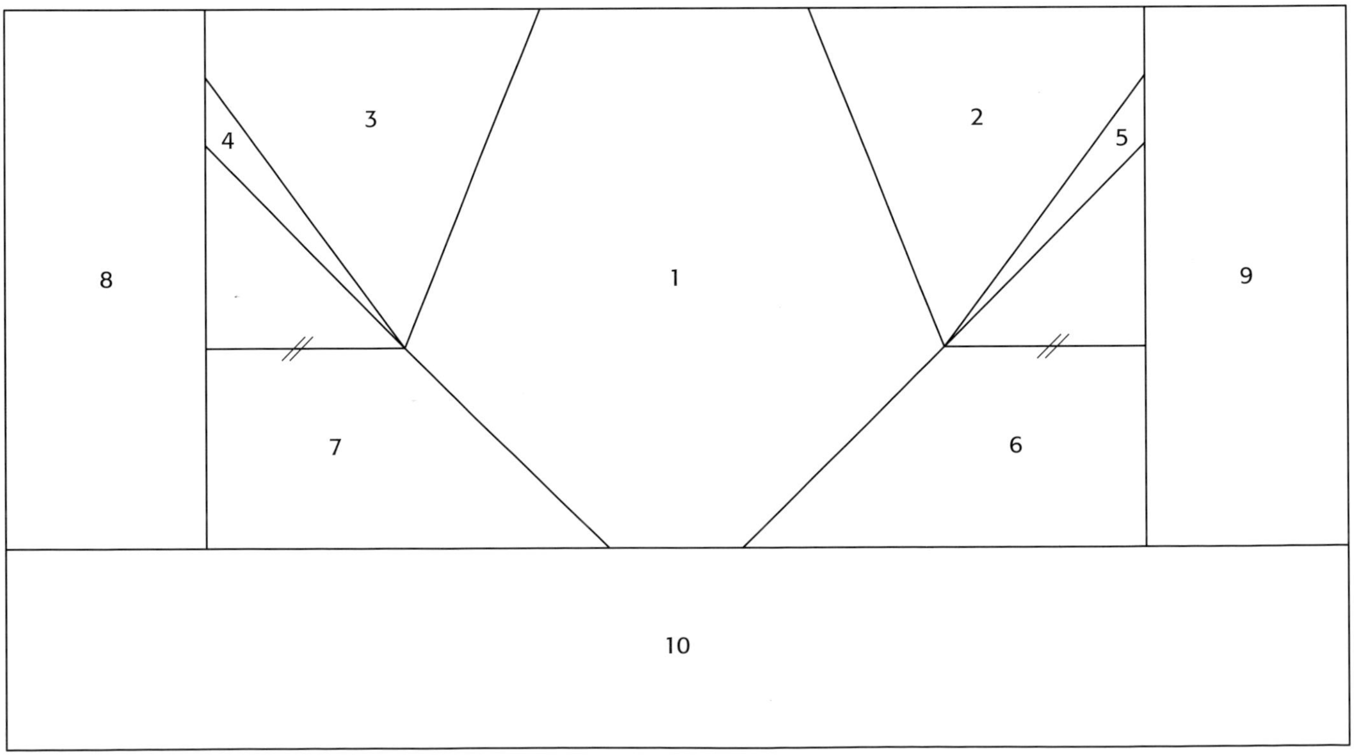

P56D

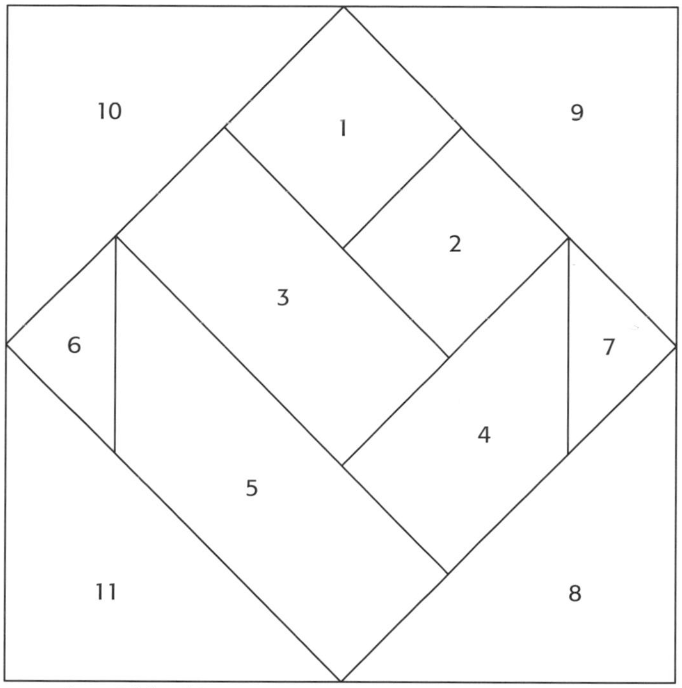

H19 (3½" block)

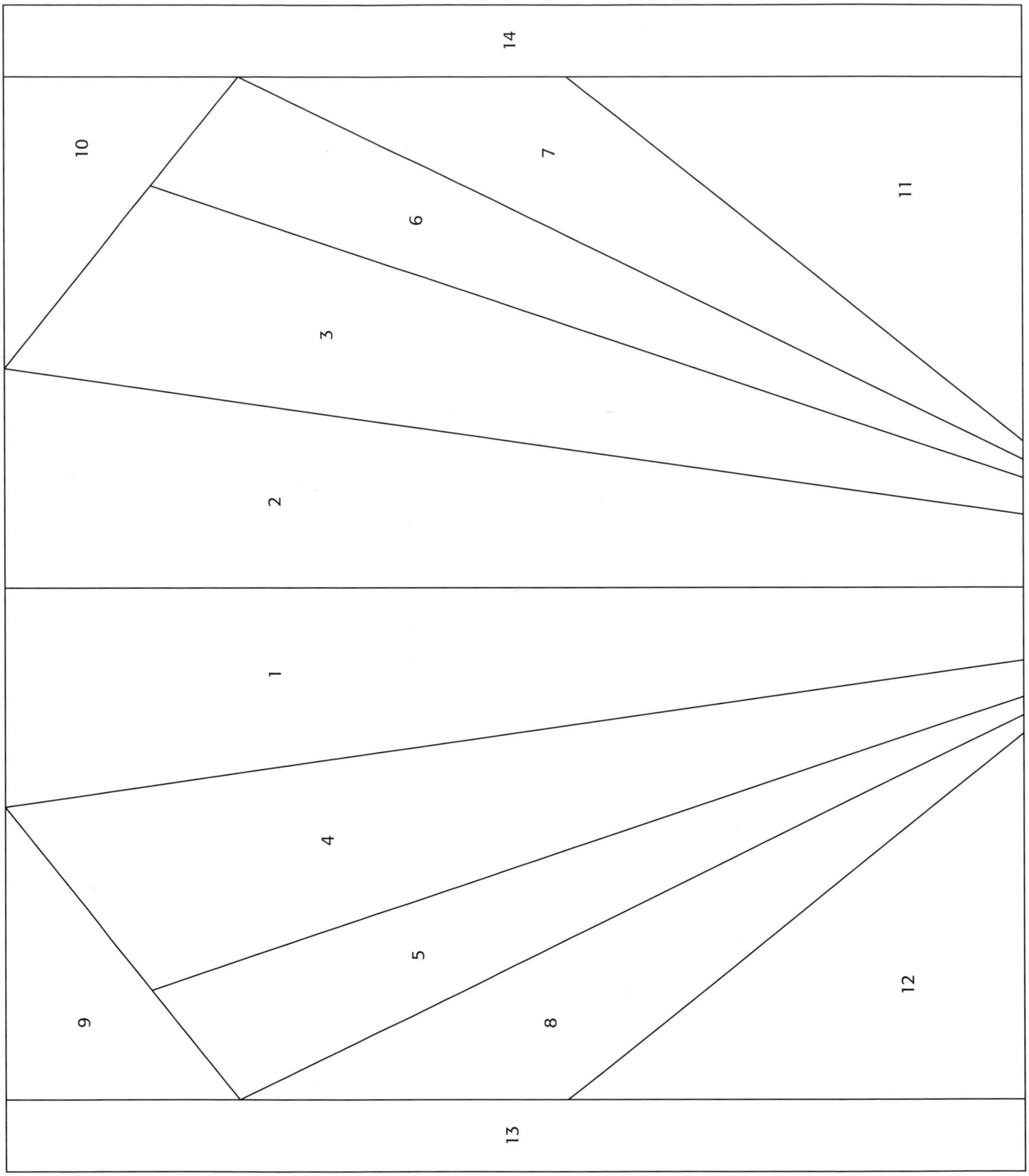

P57A

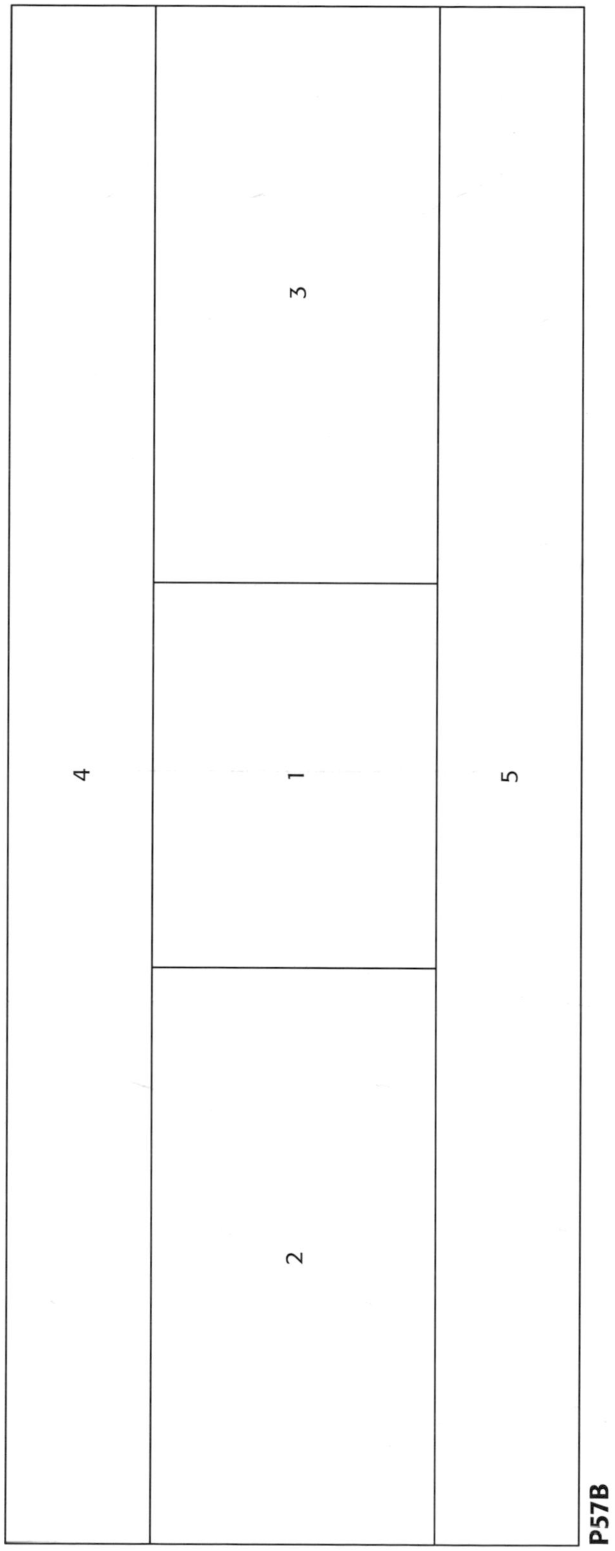
4
1
5
3
2
P57B

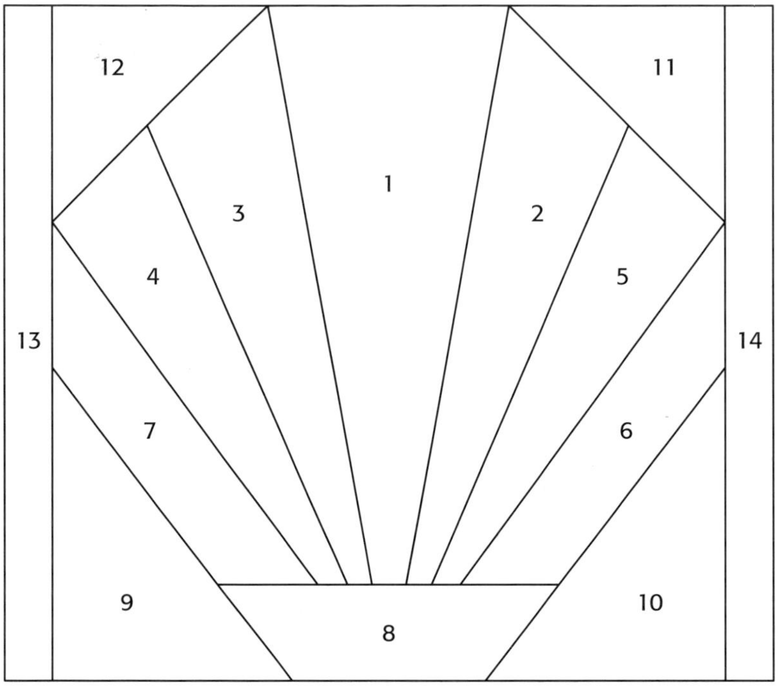

P58A

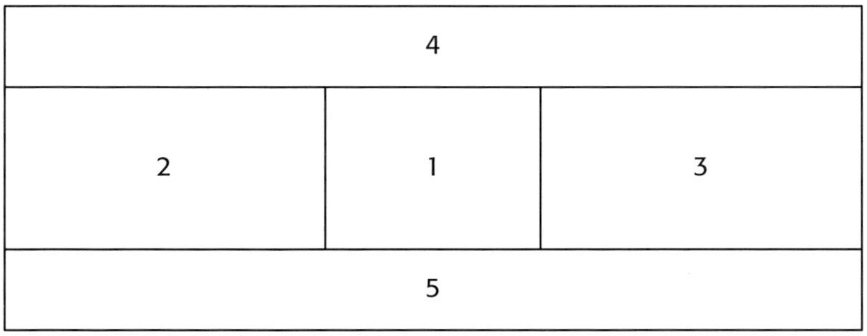

P58B

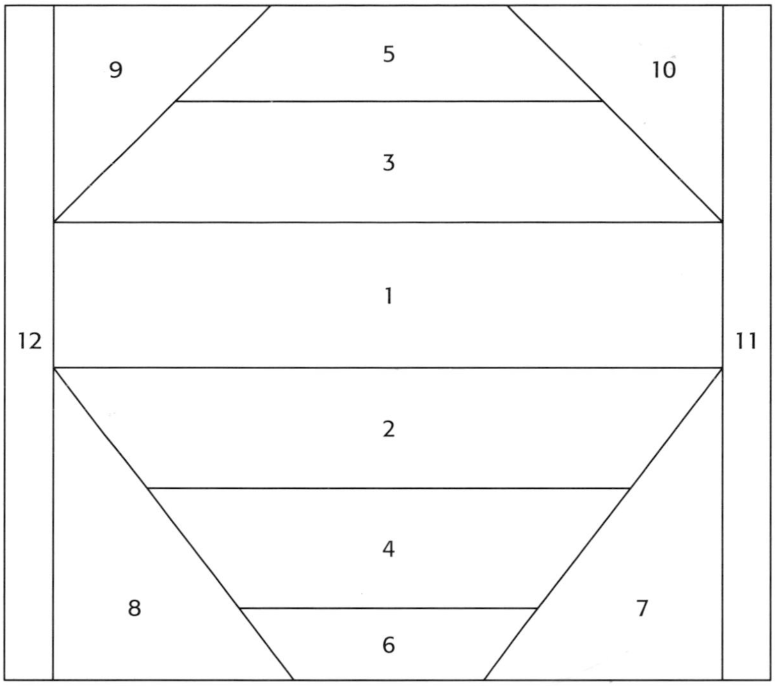

P59A

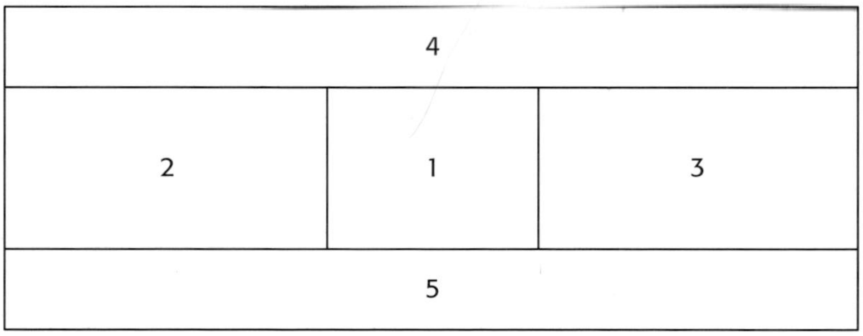

P59B

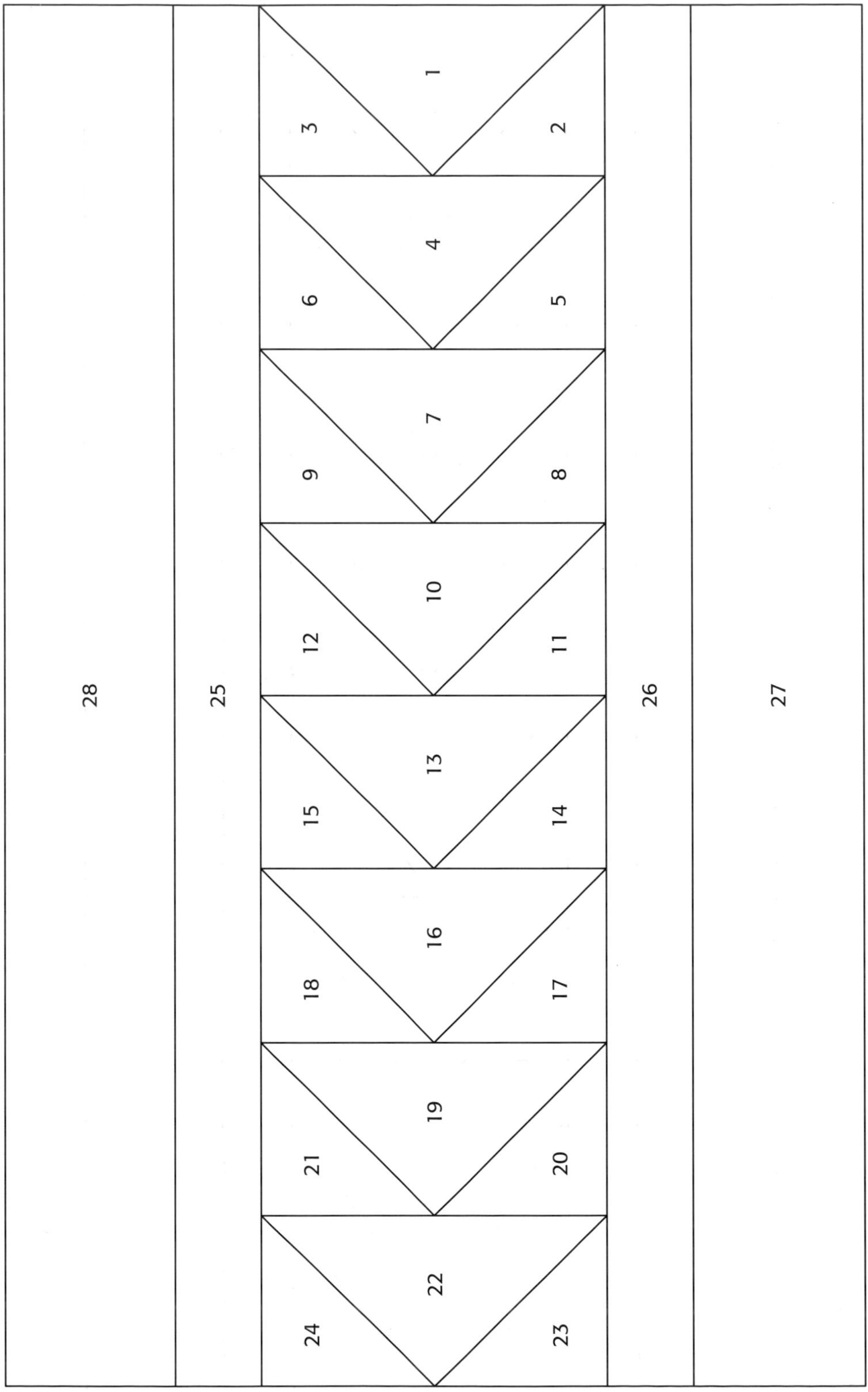

PB12

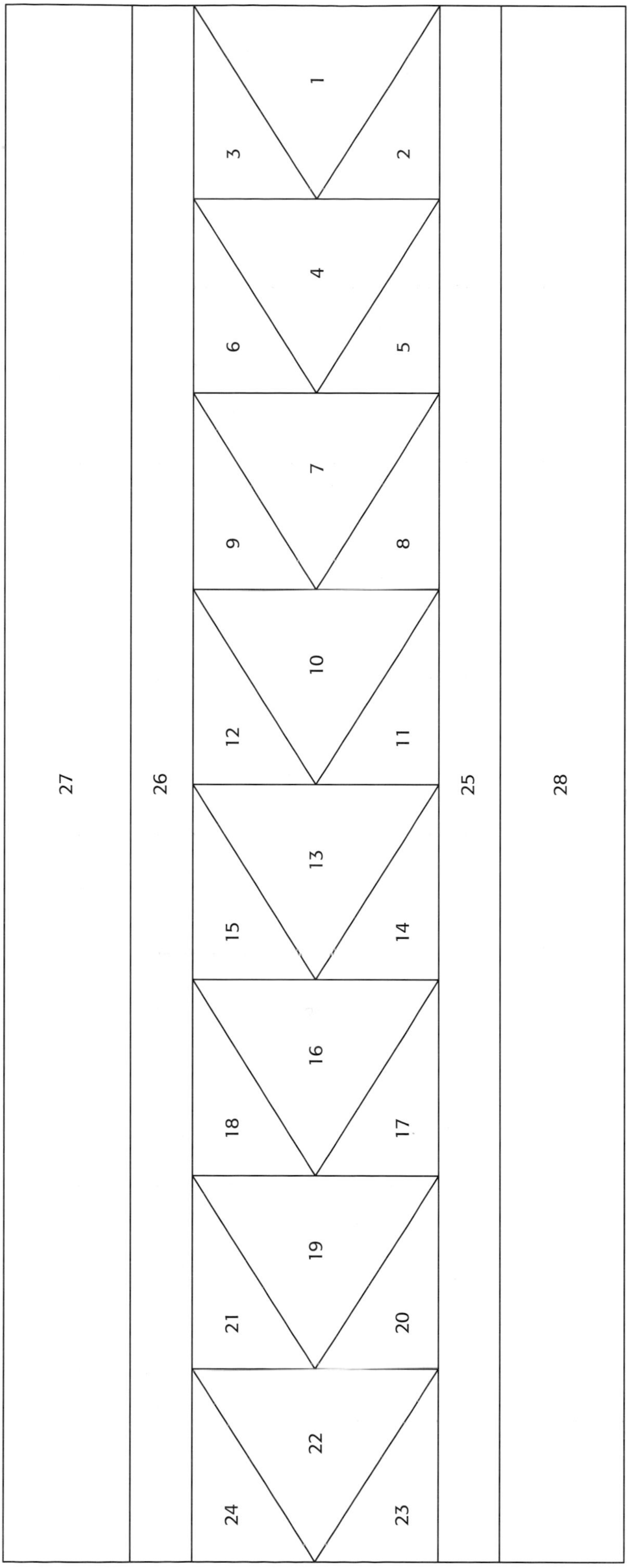

PB13

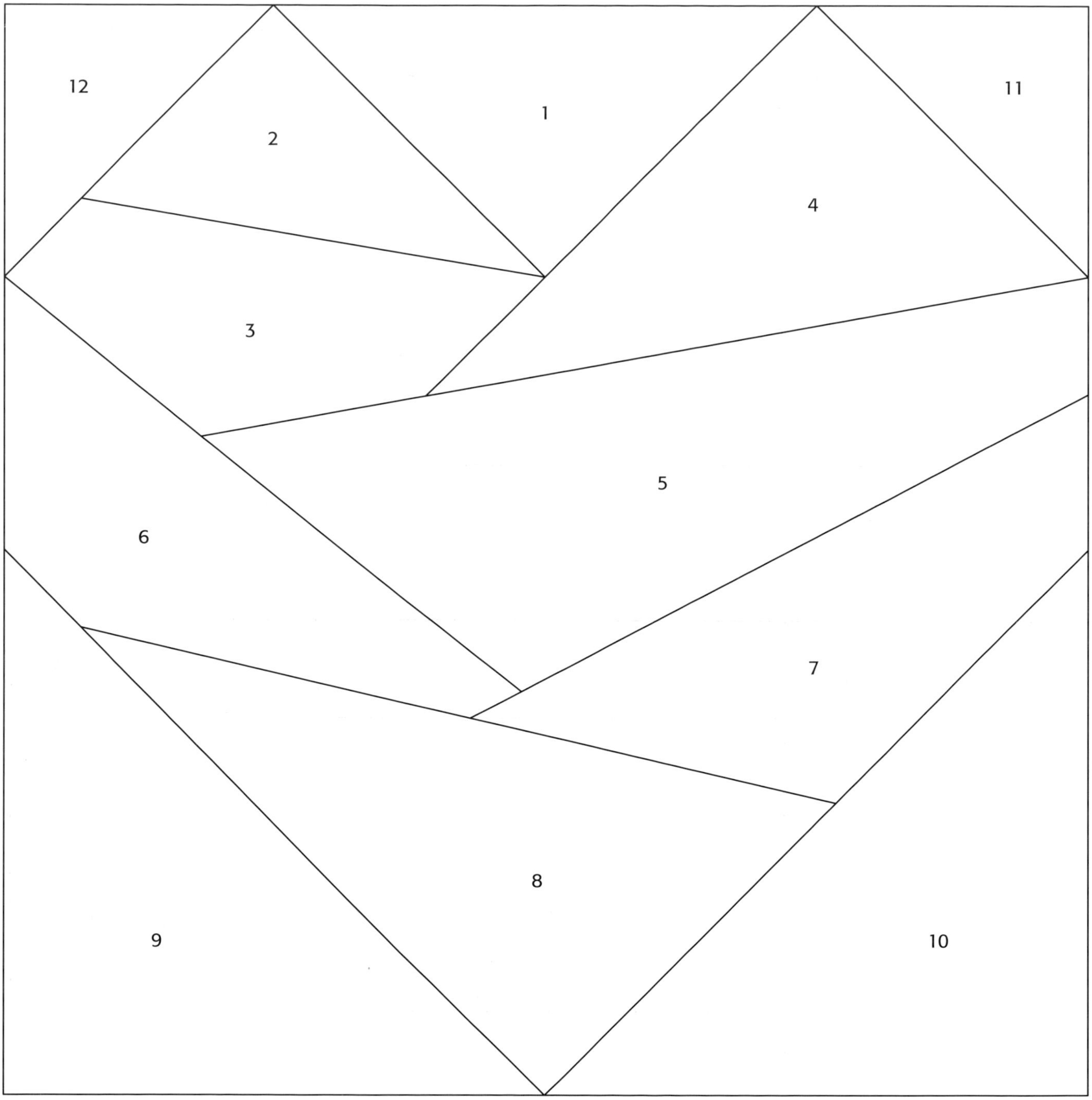

H20

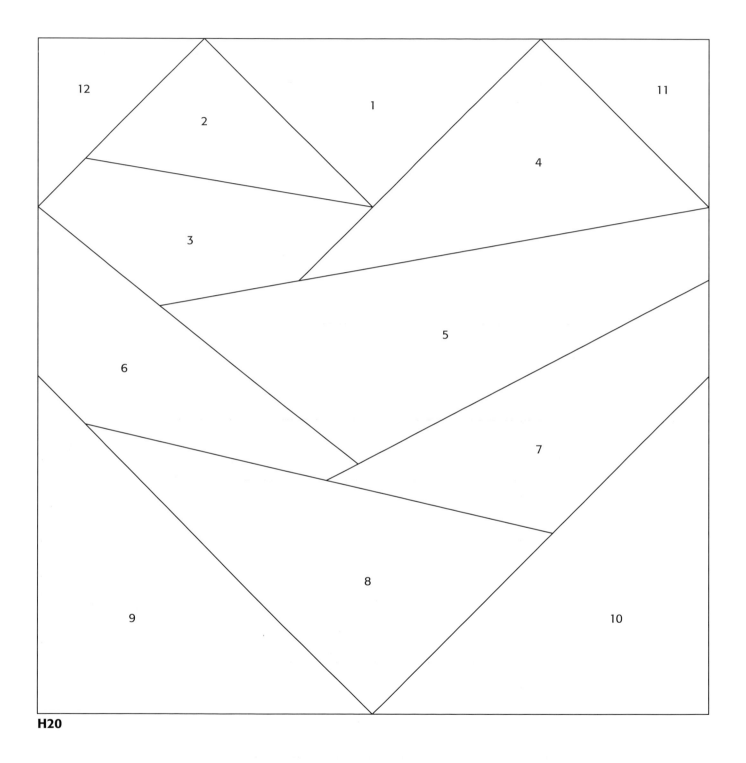

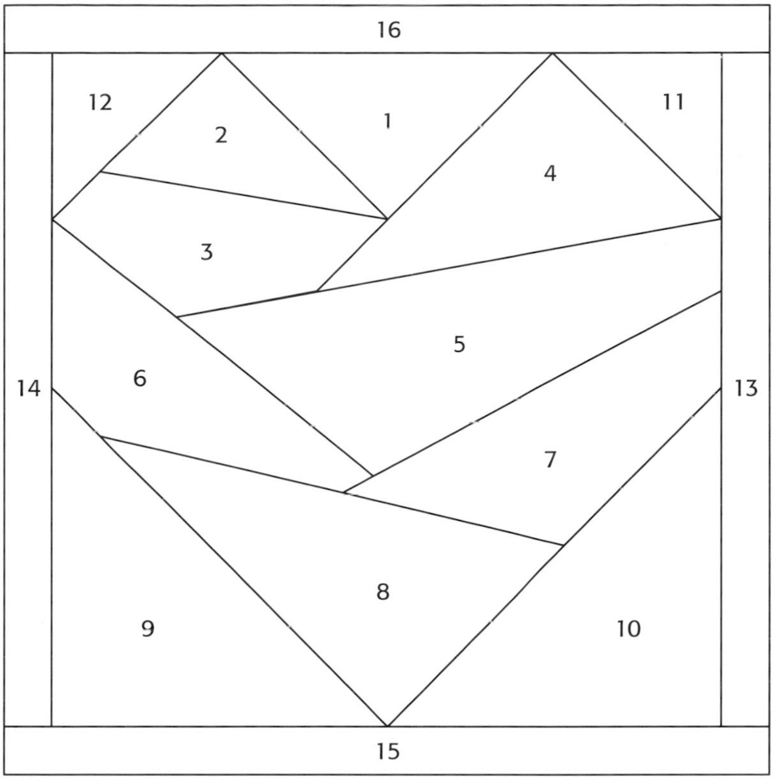

H21

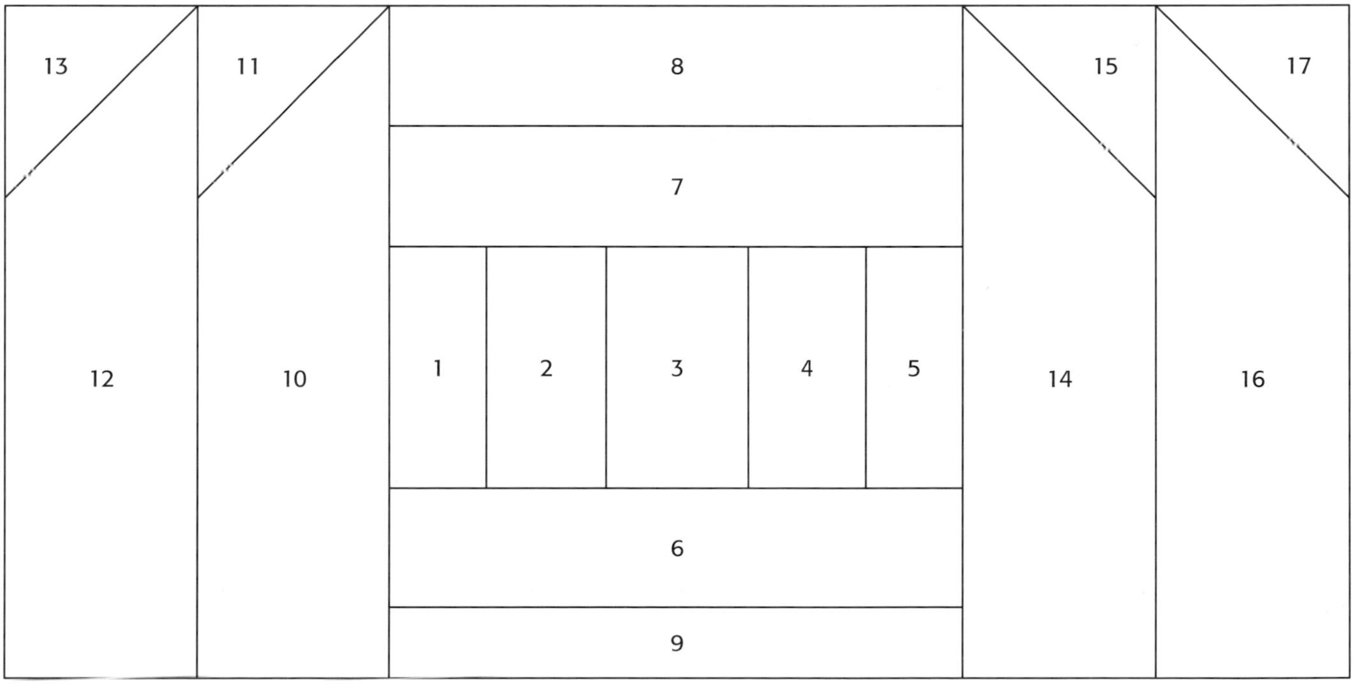

P62

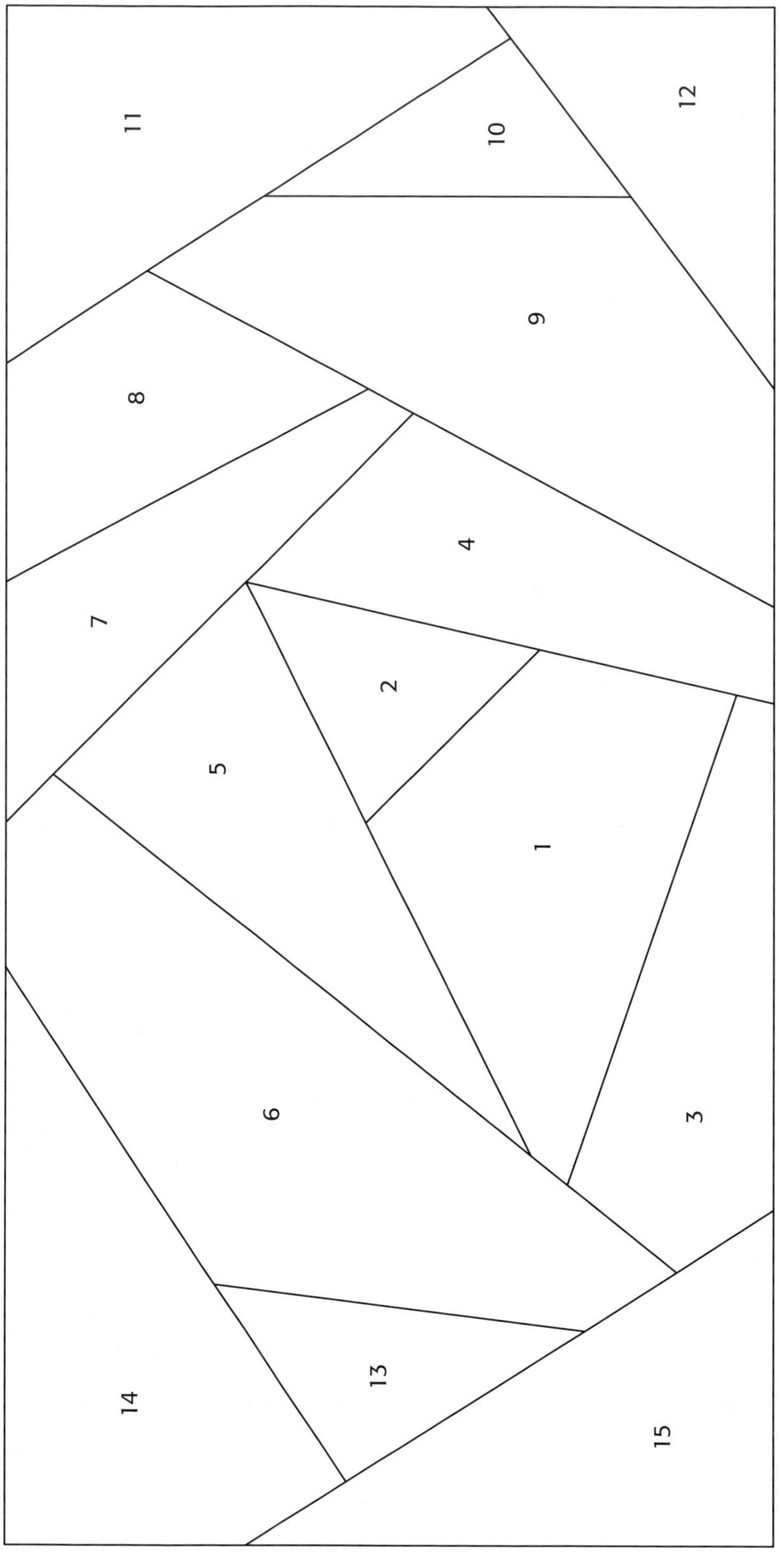

PB14

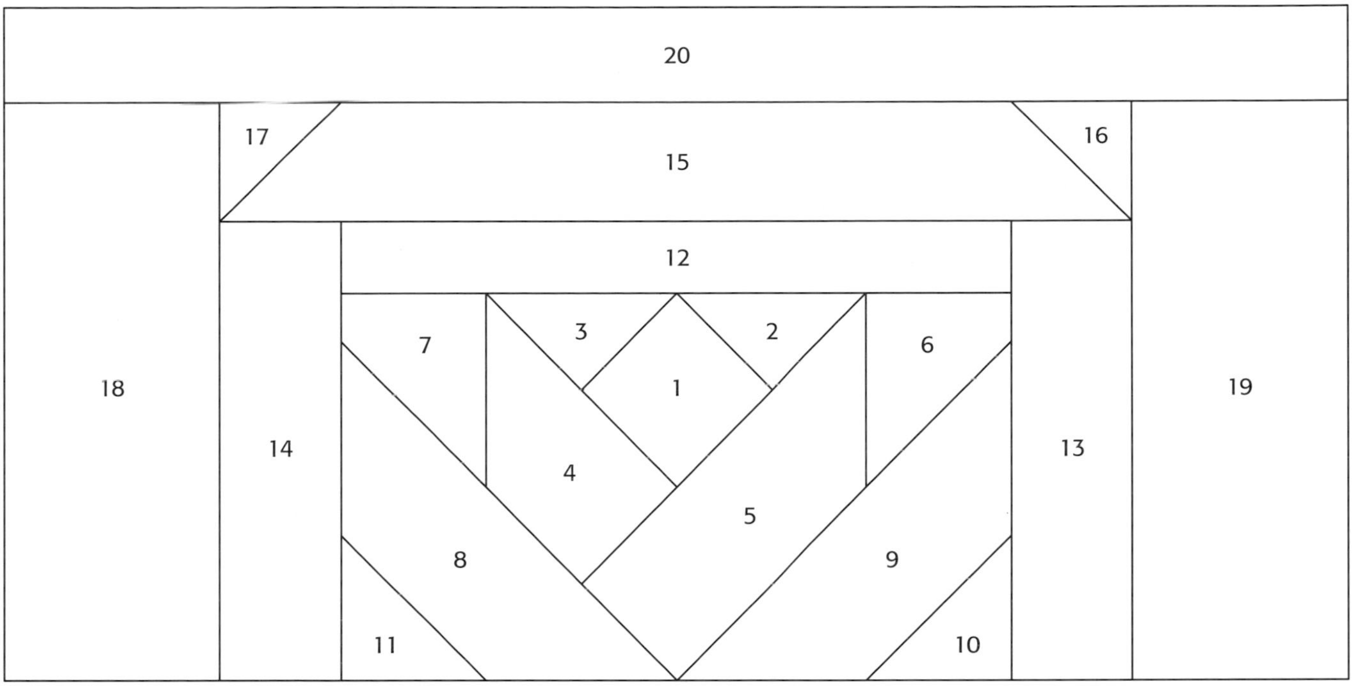

B18A

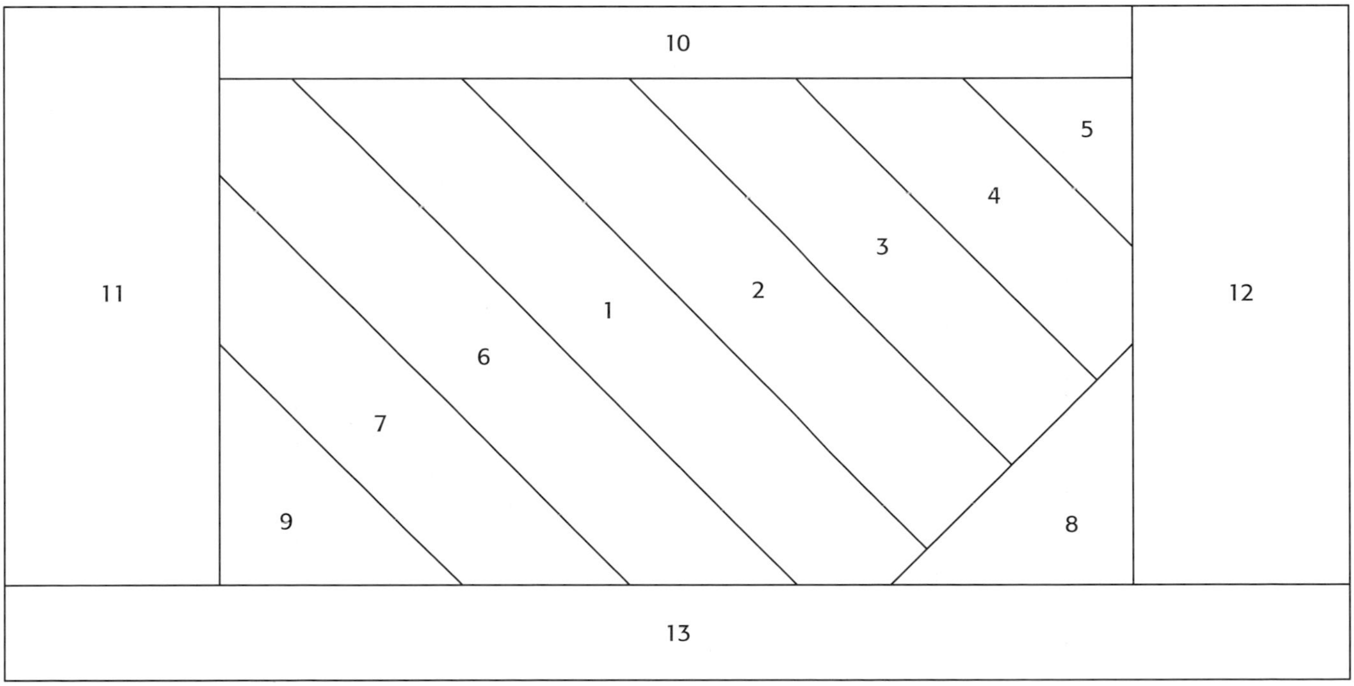

B18B

G90

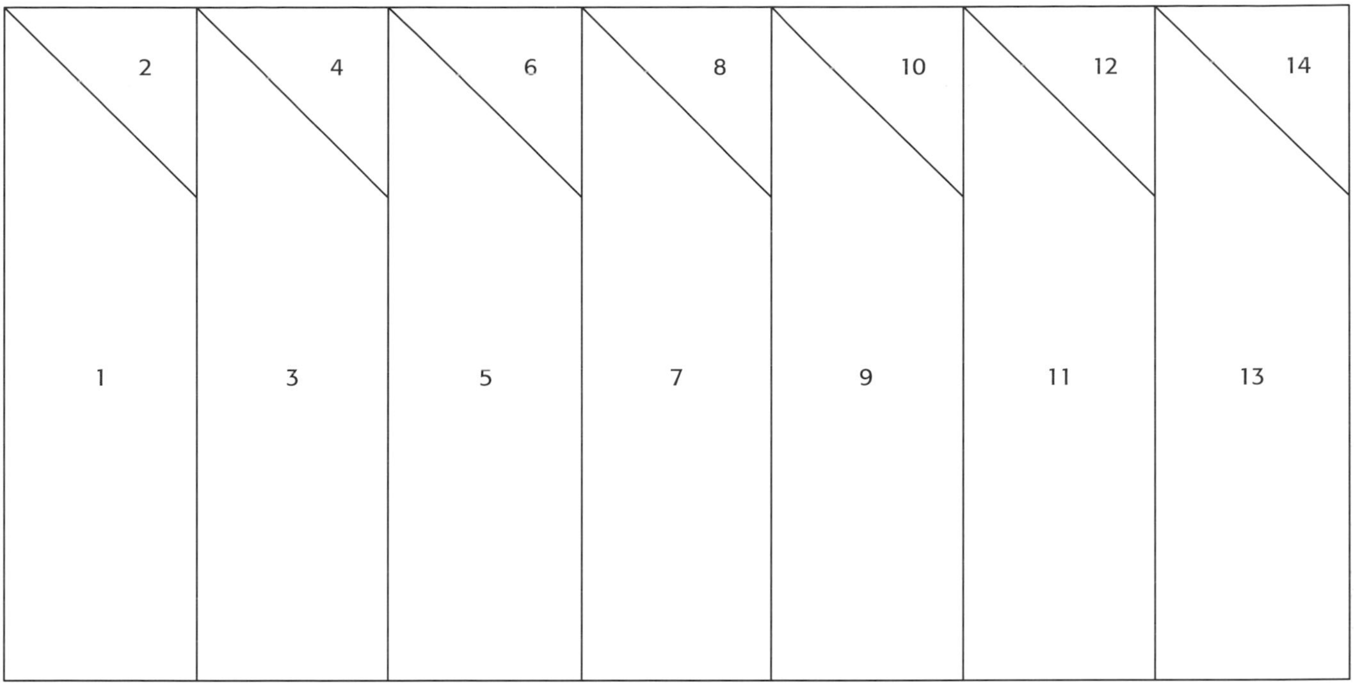

P60

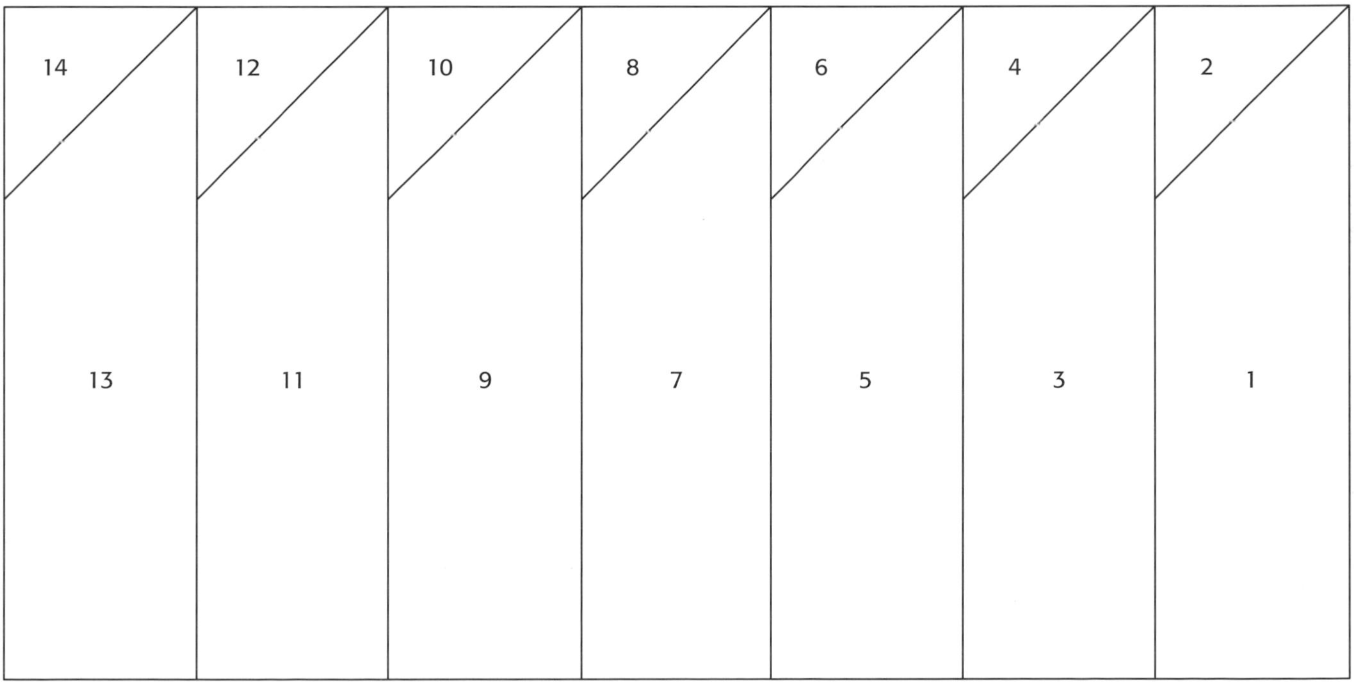

P61

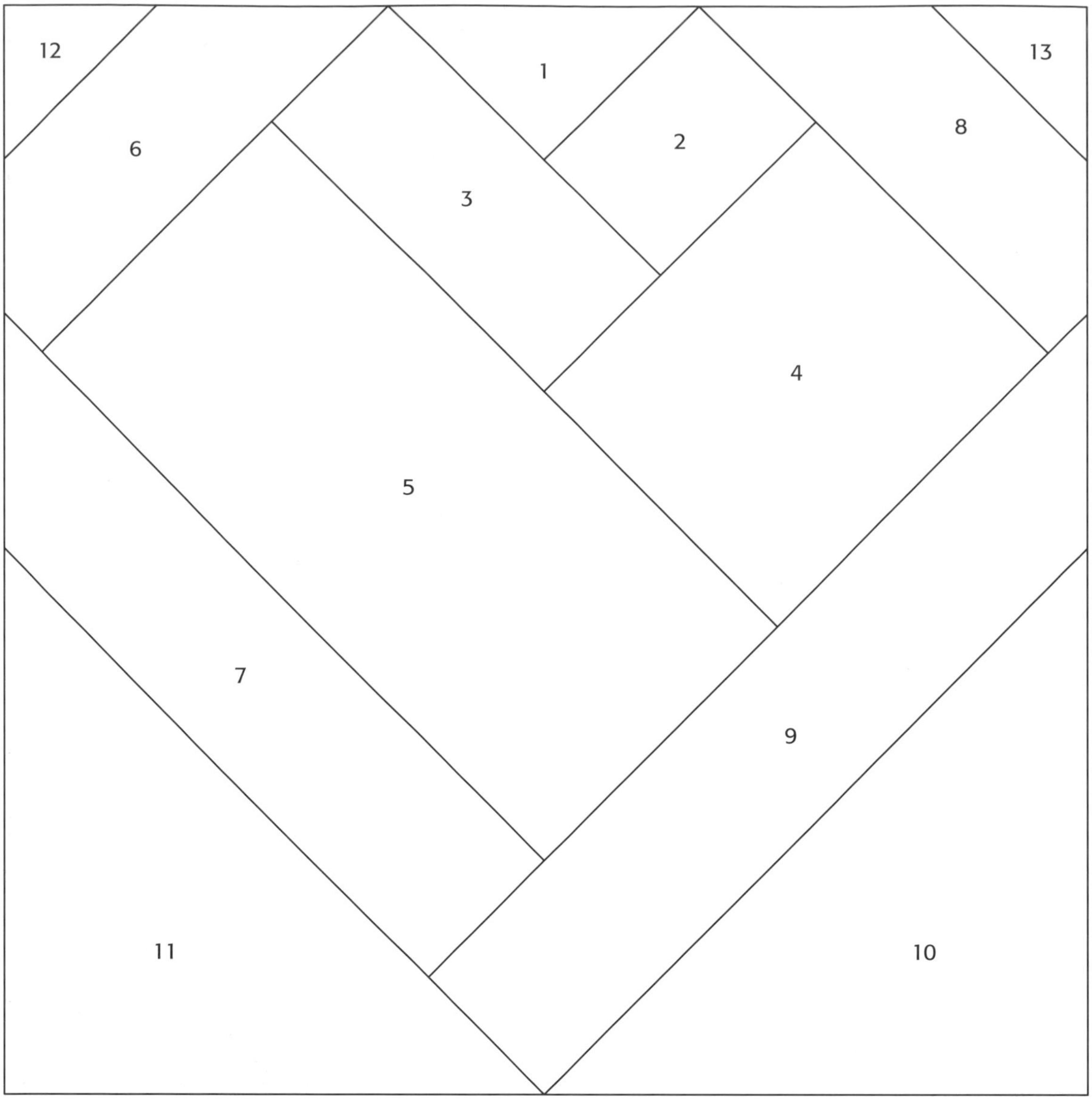

H22

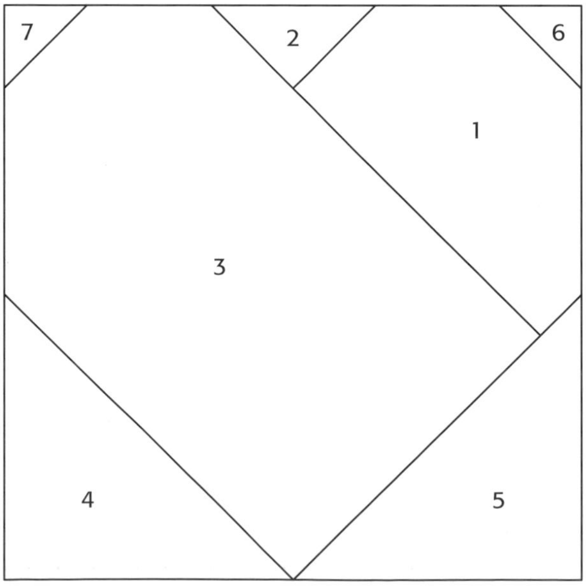

H23

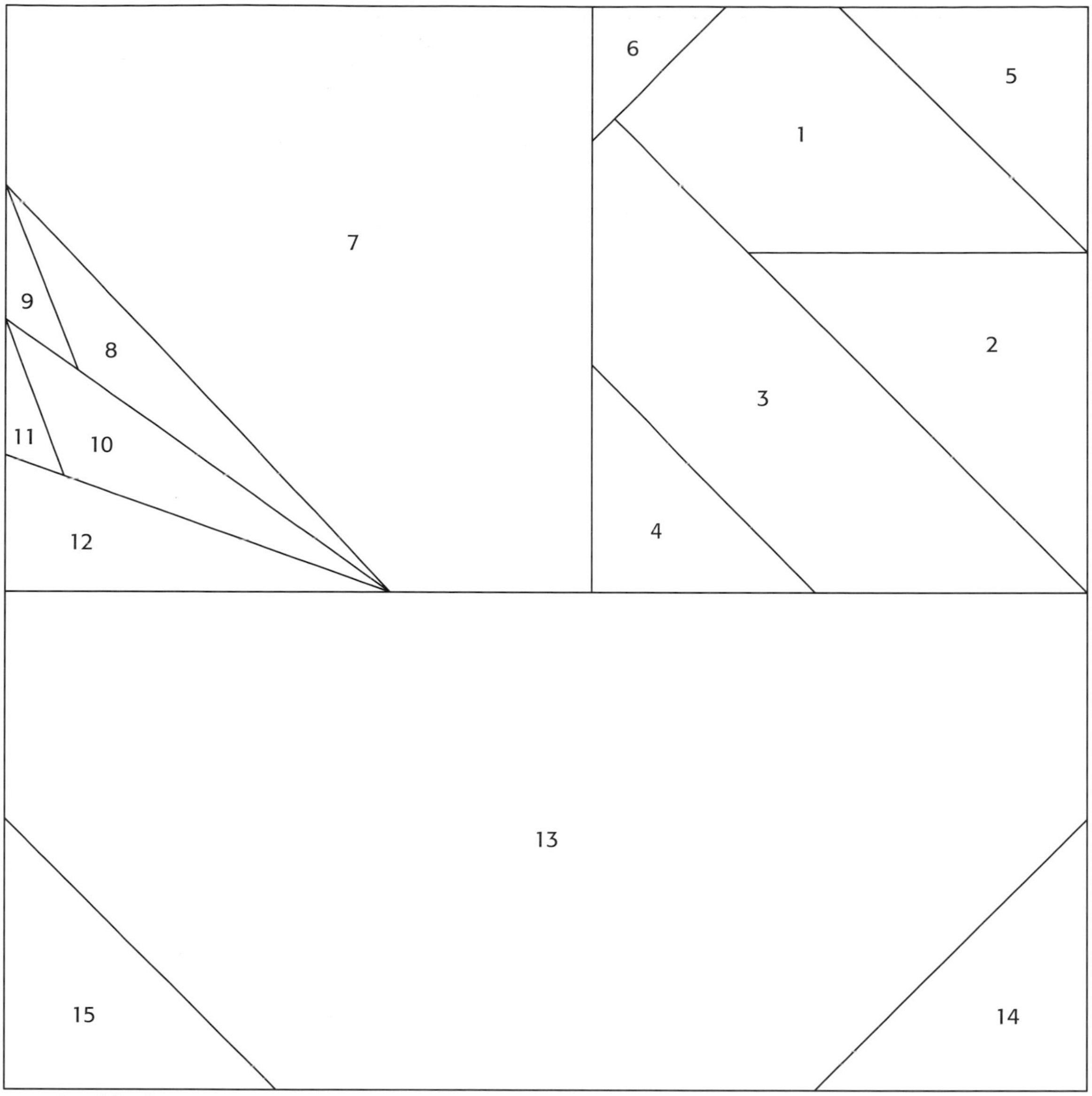

P63 (6" block)

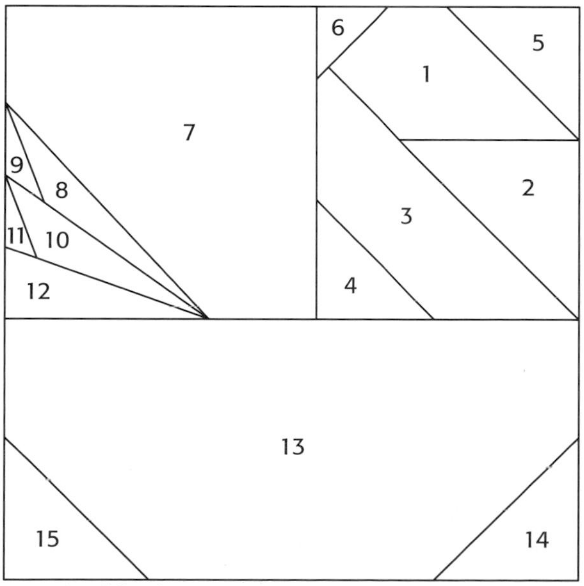

P63 (3" block)

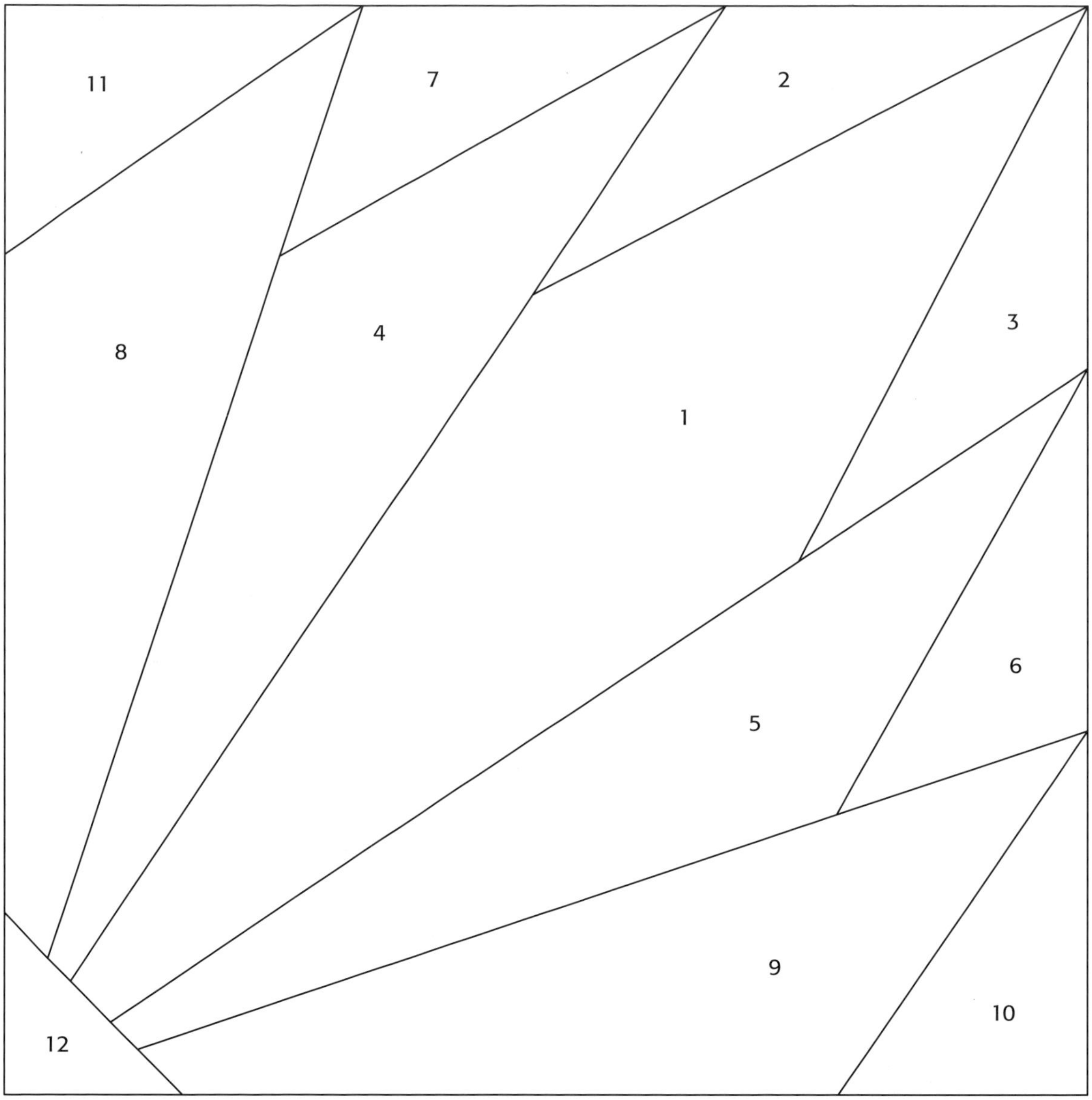

G91

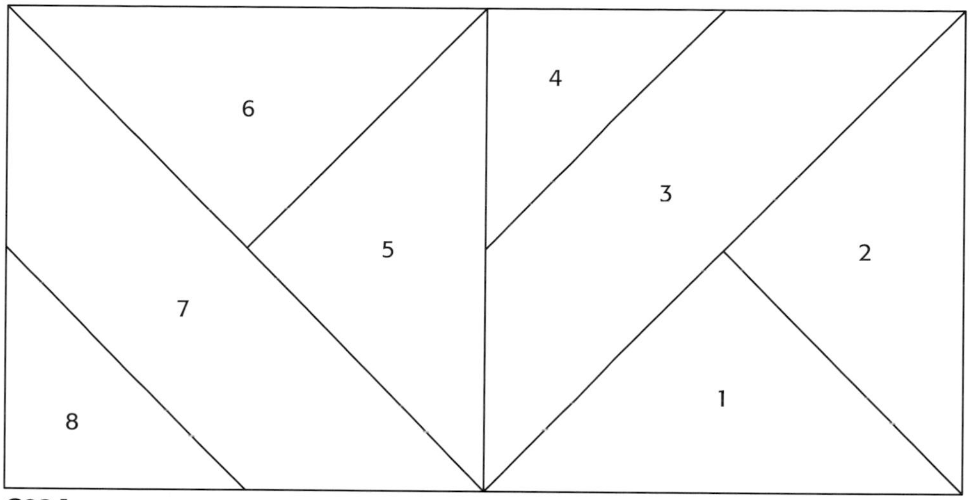

G92A

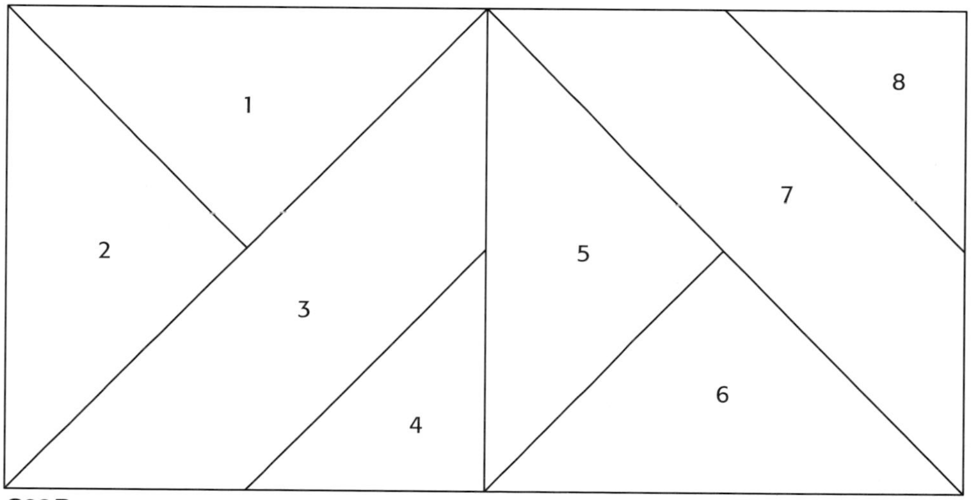

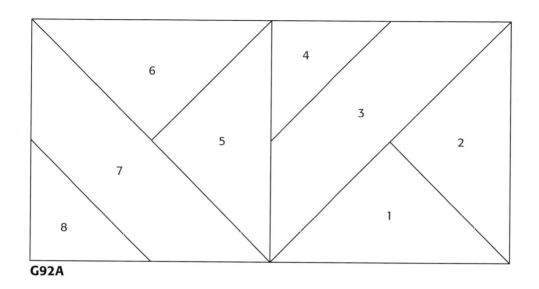

G92B

P64C

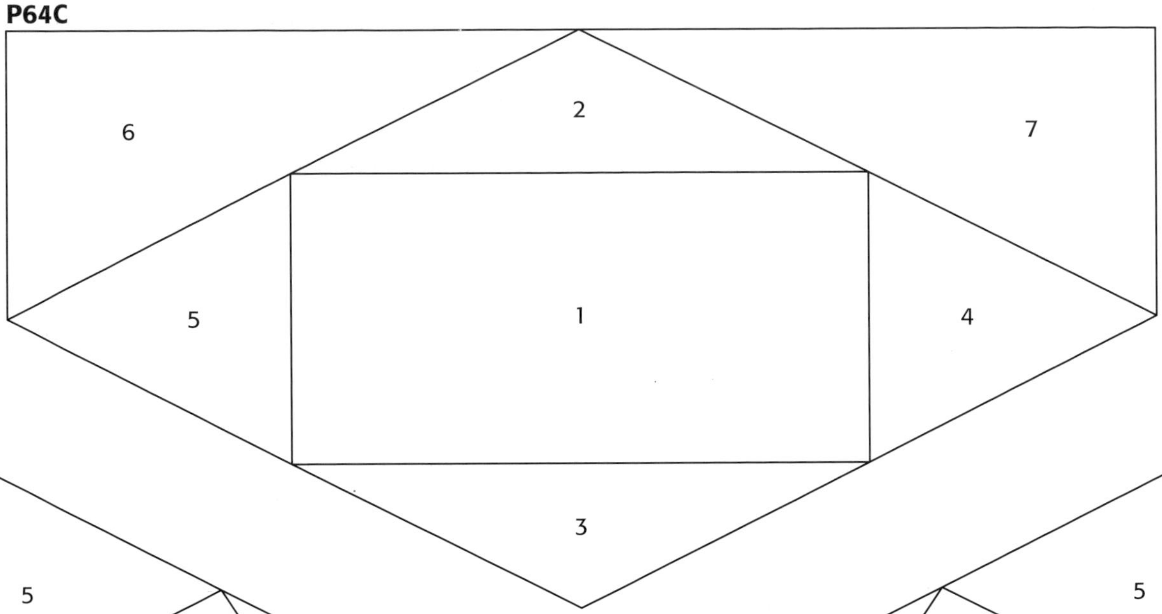

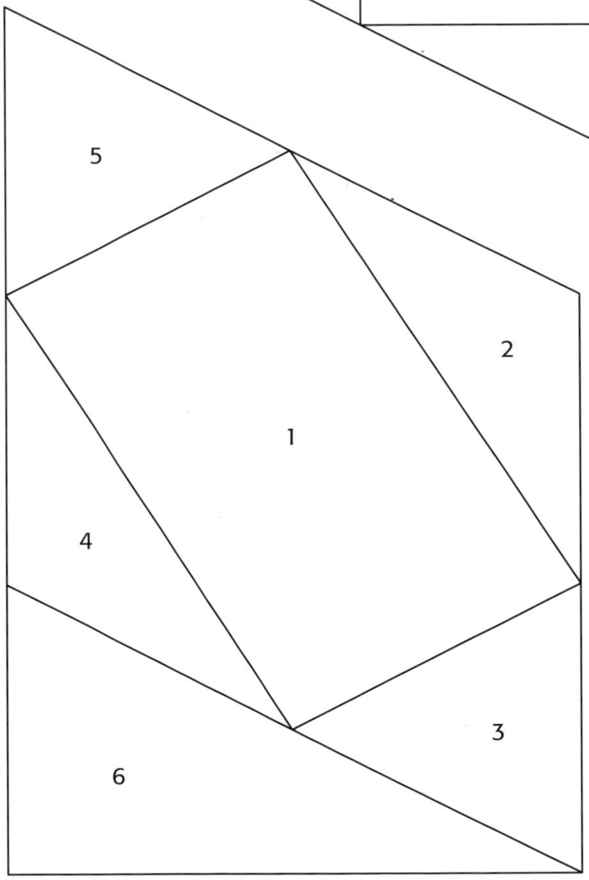

P64A

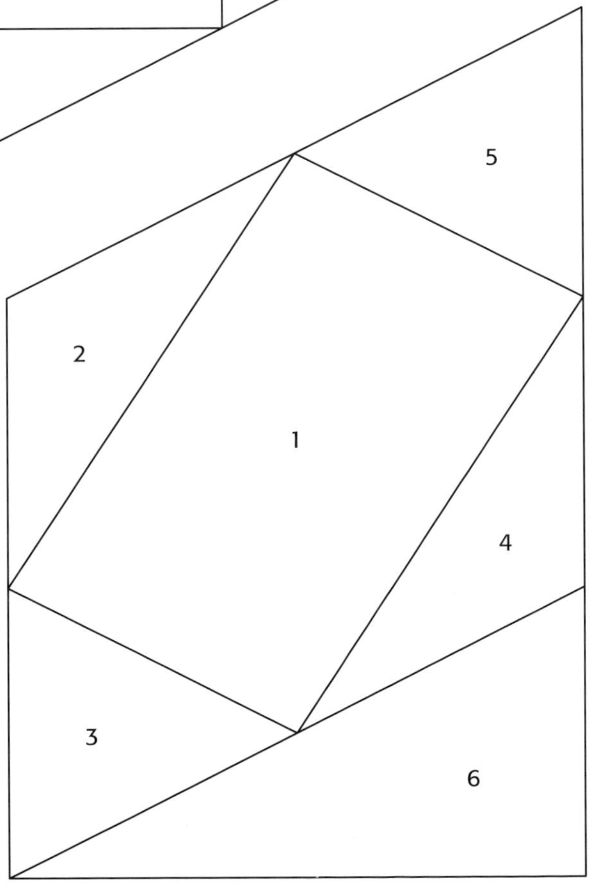

P64B

P65A

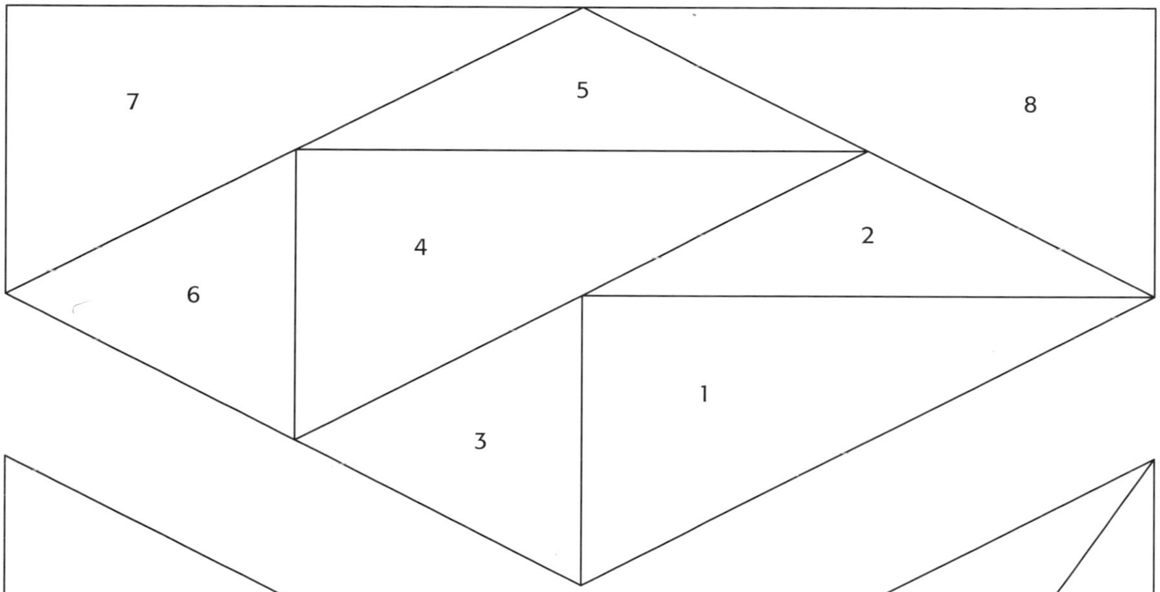

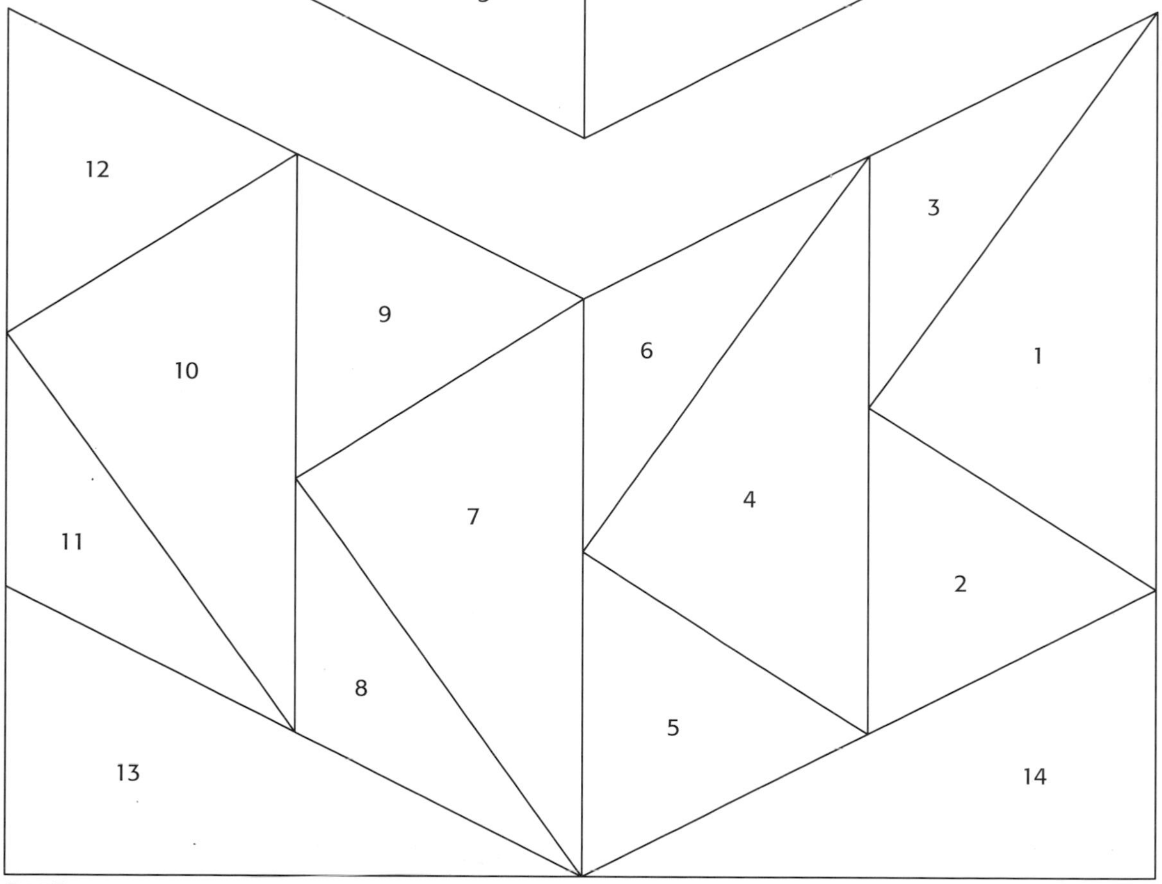

P65B

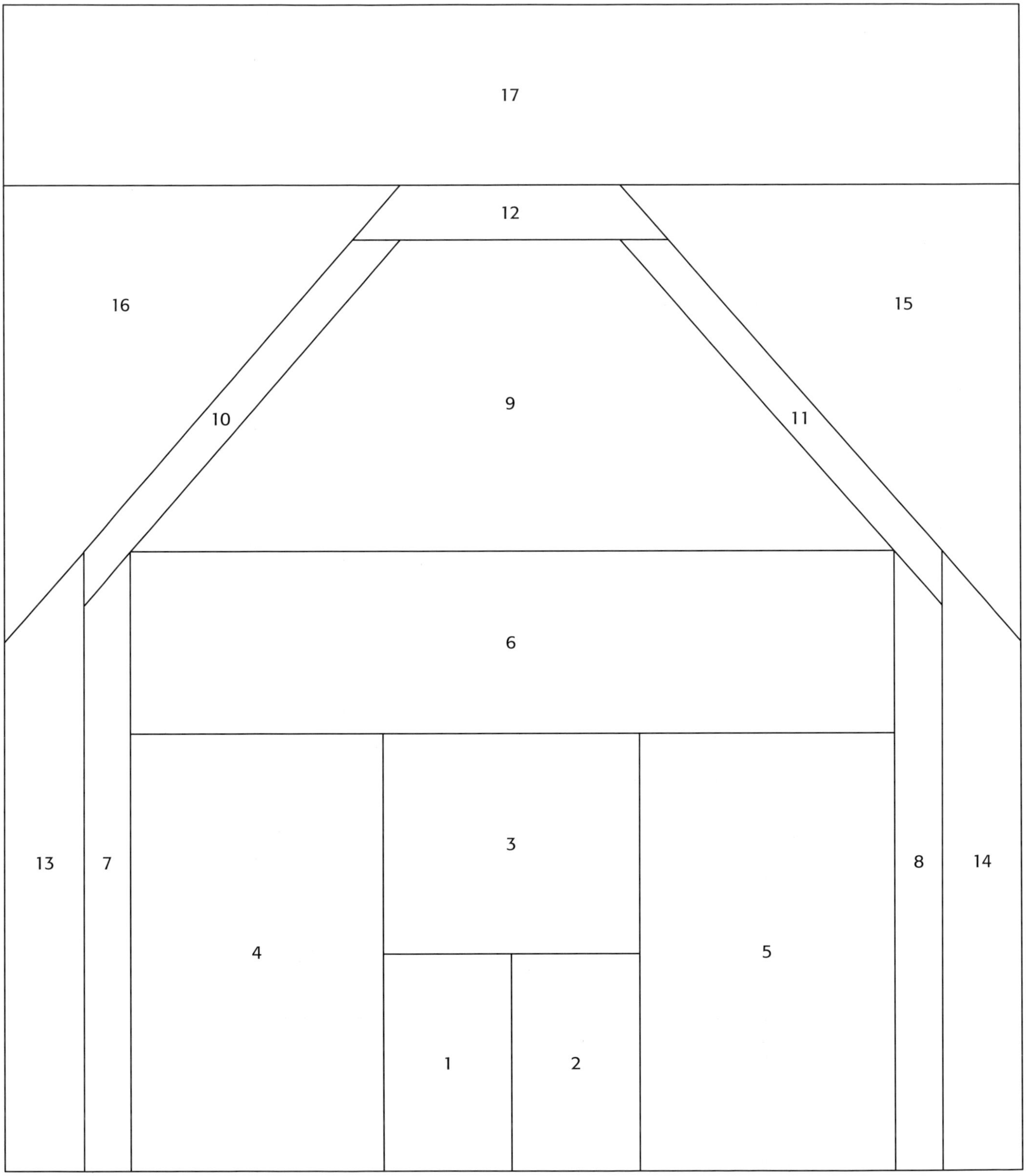

P66

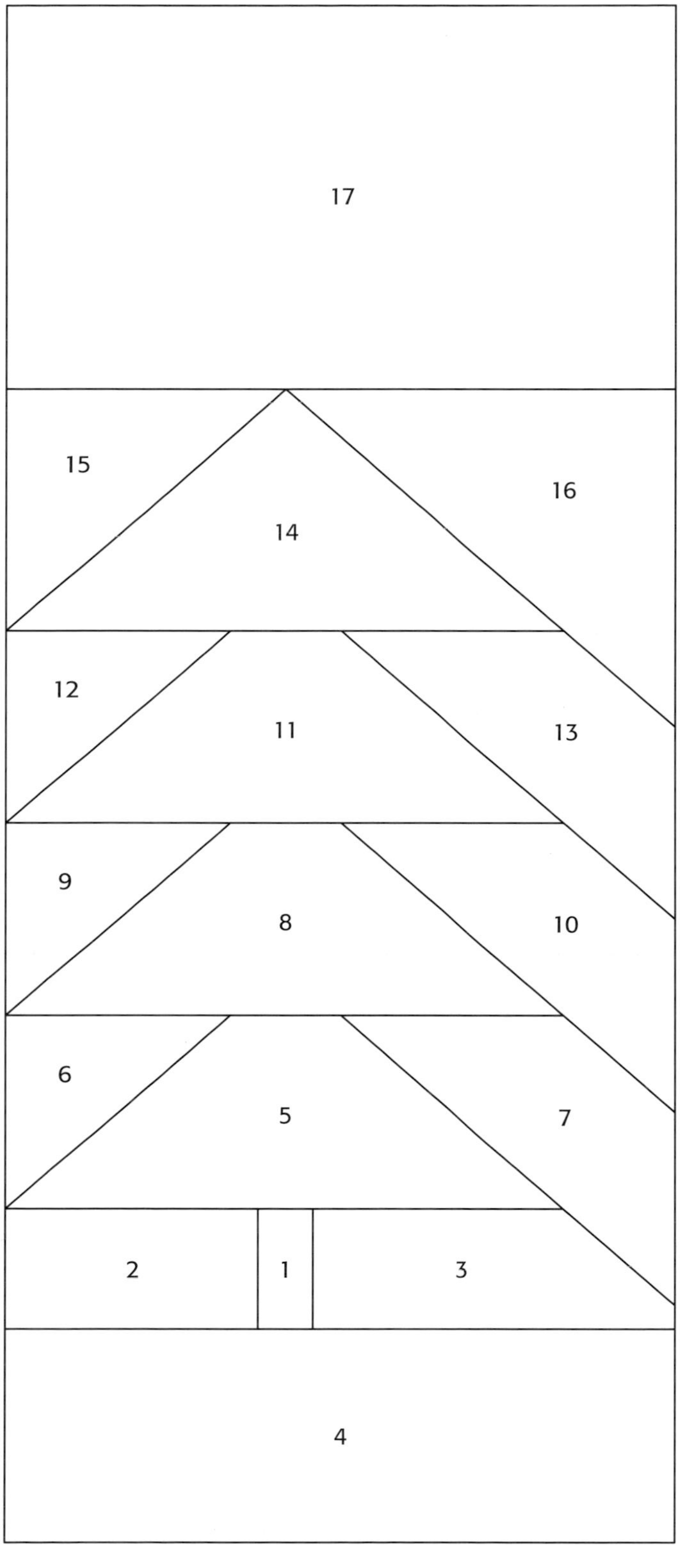

T21

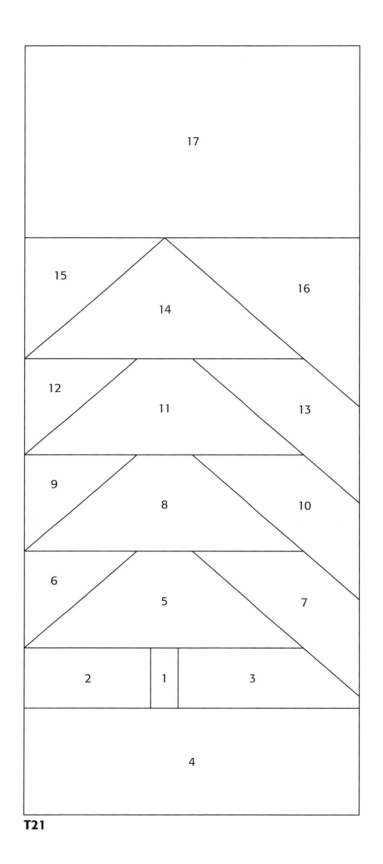

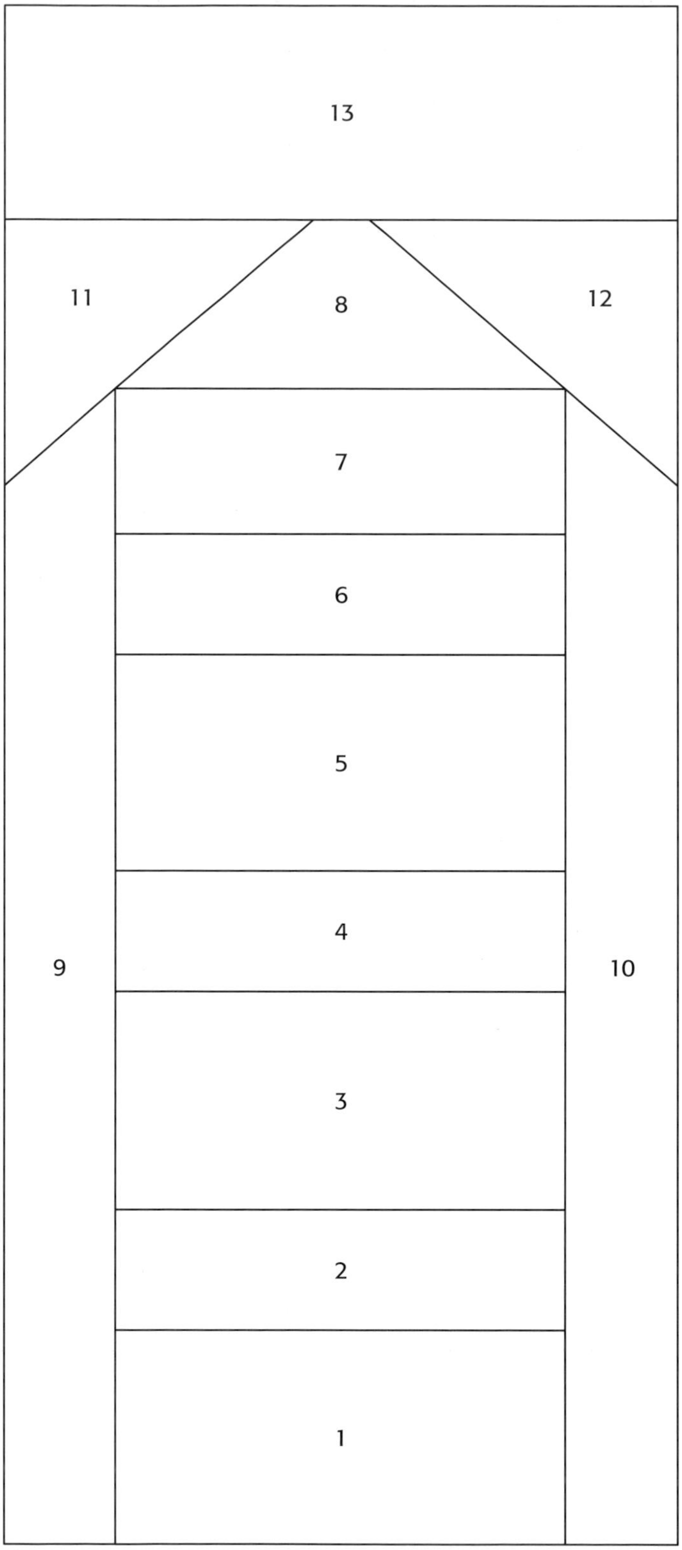

P67

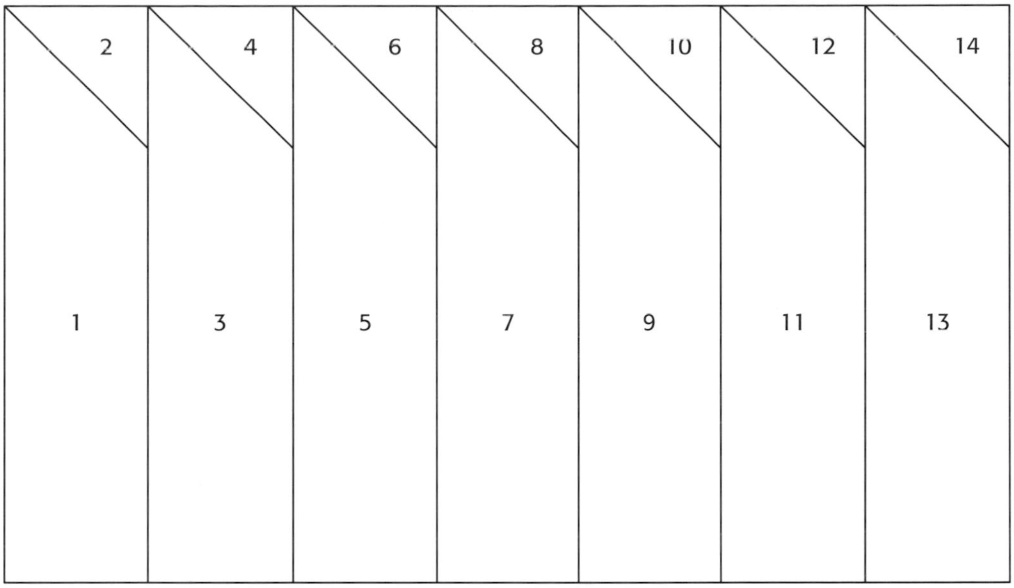

P68

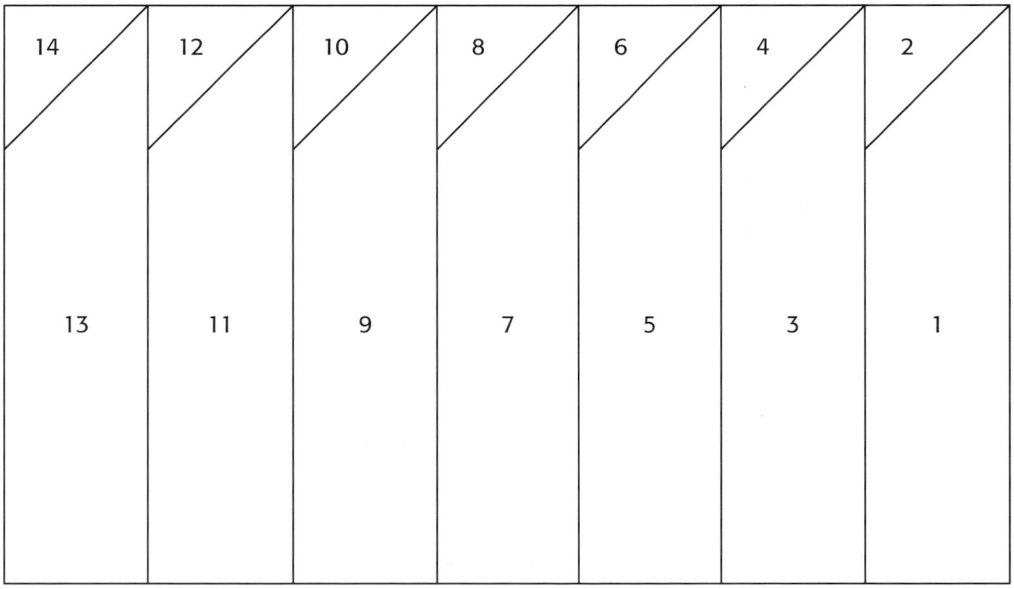

P69

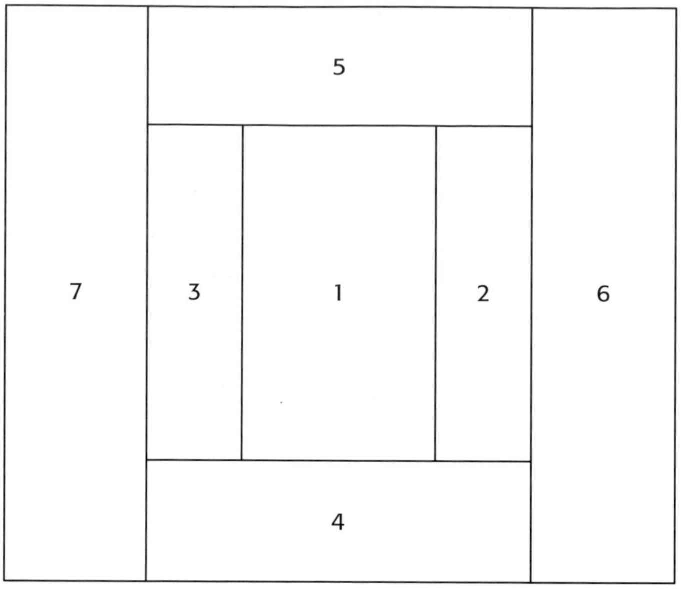

P70

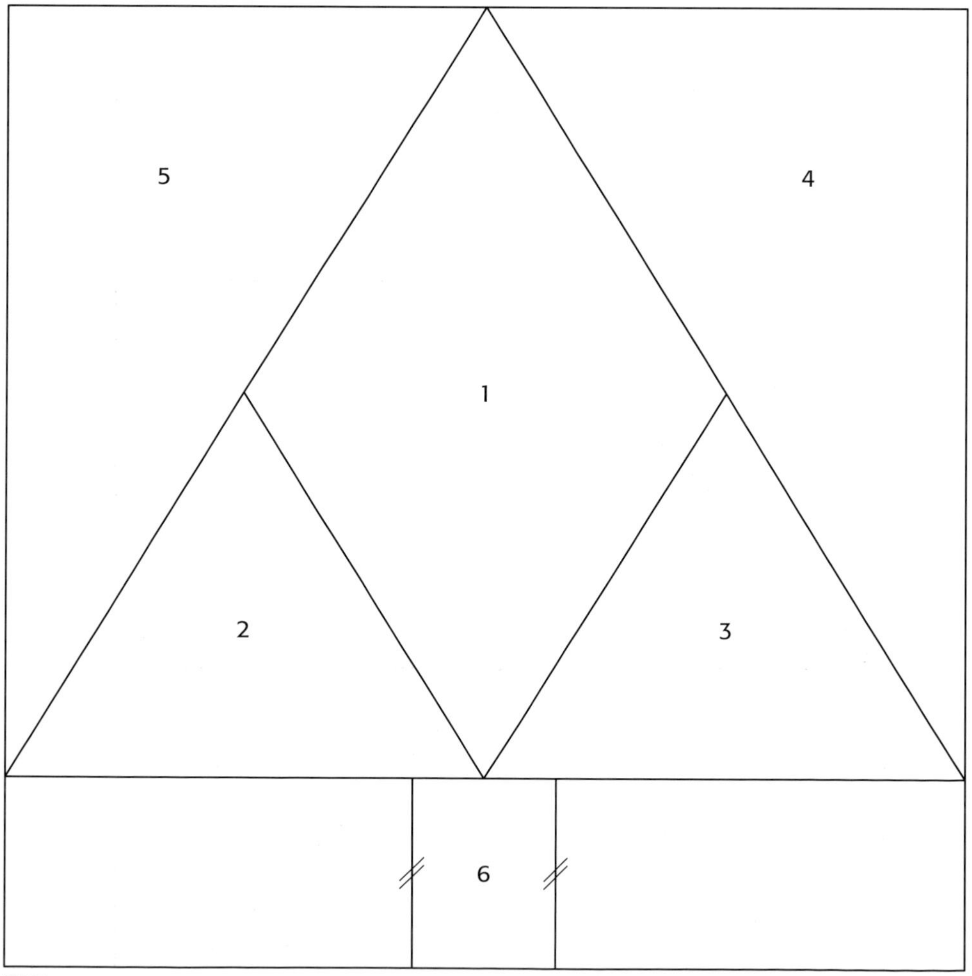

T22

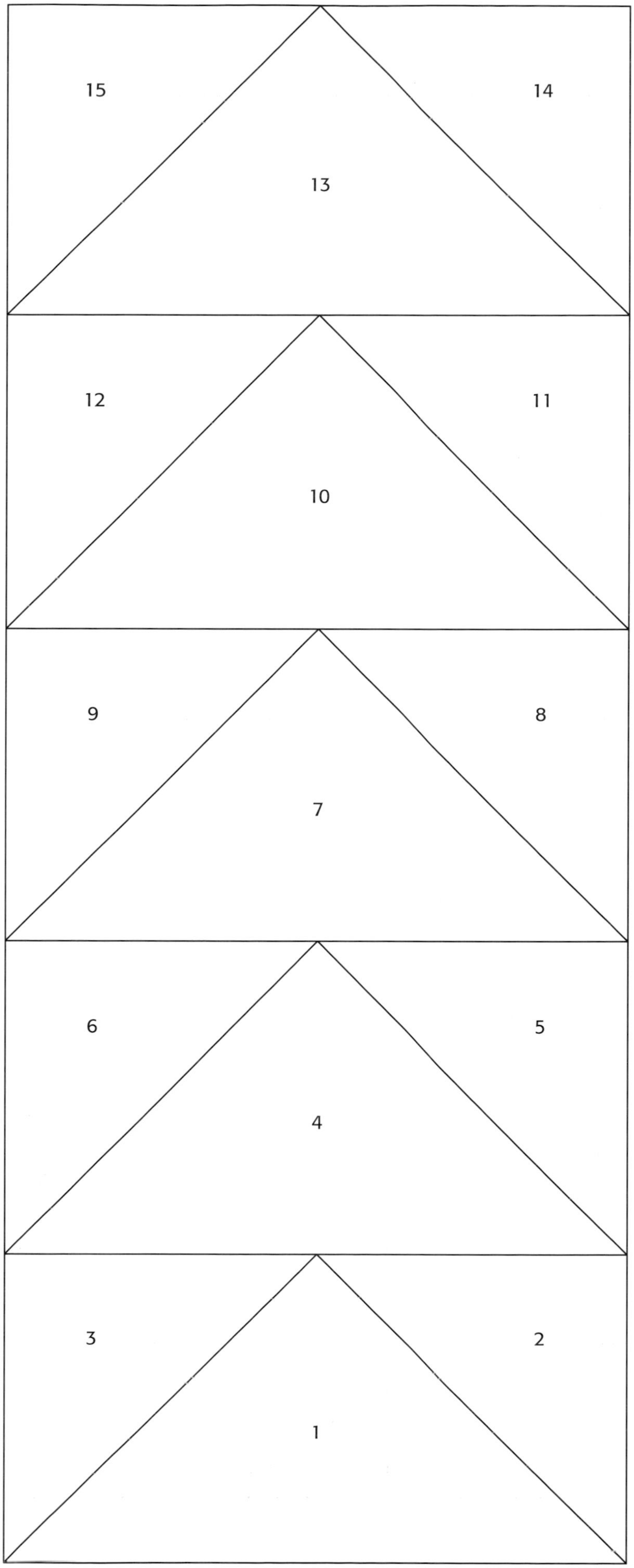

PB15

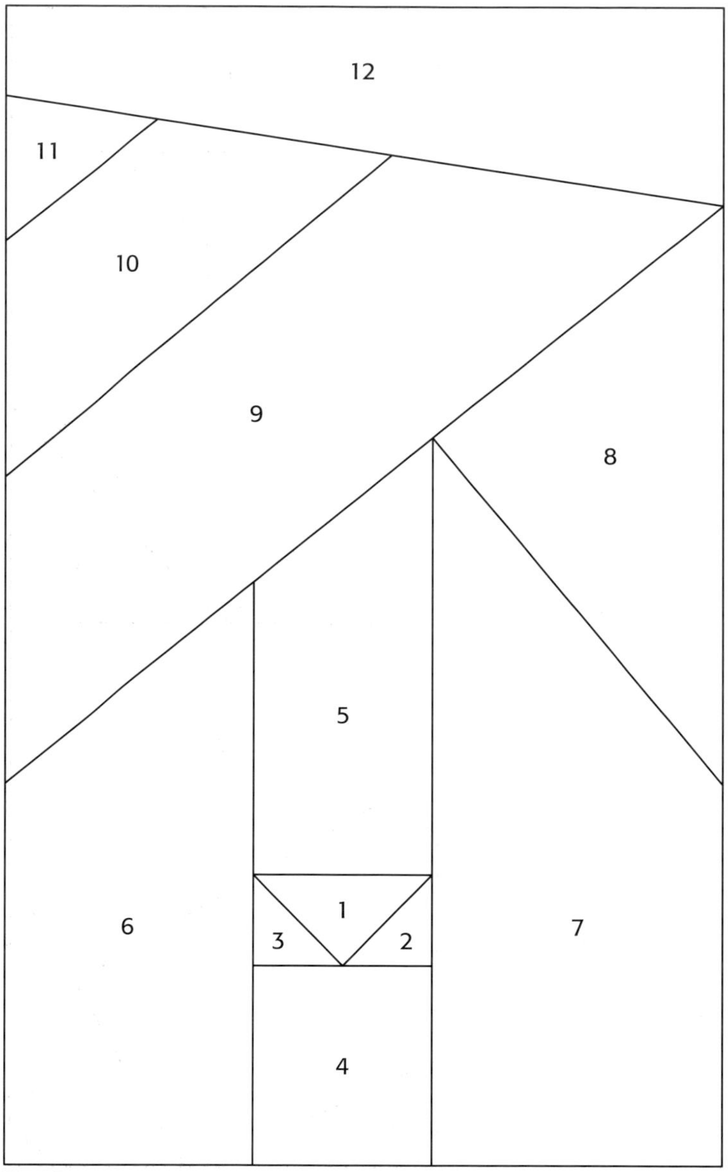

P71A

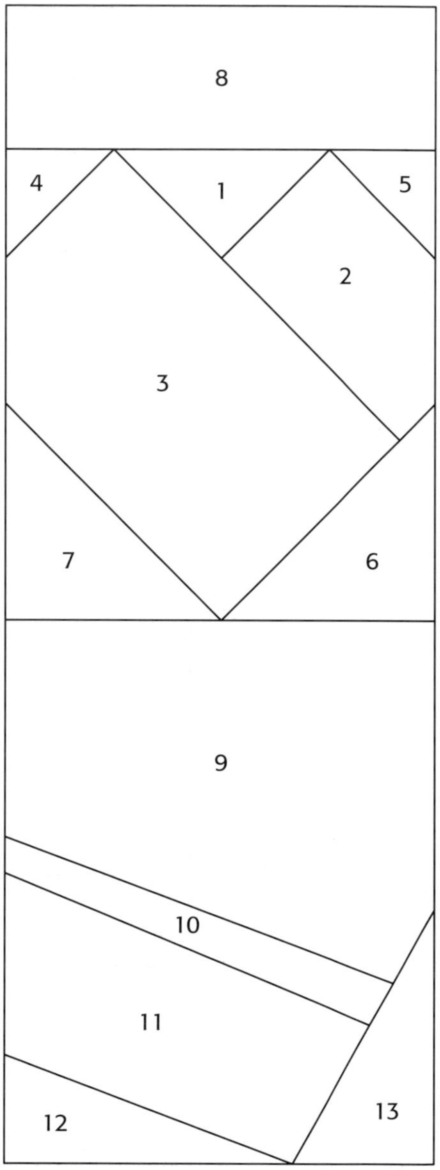

P71B

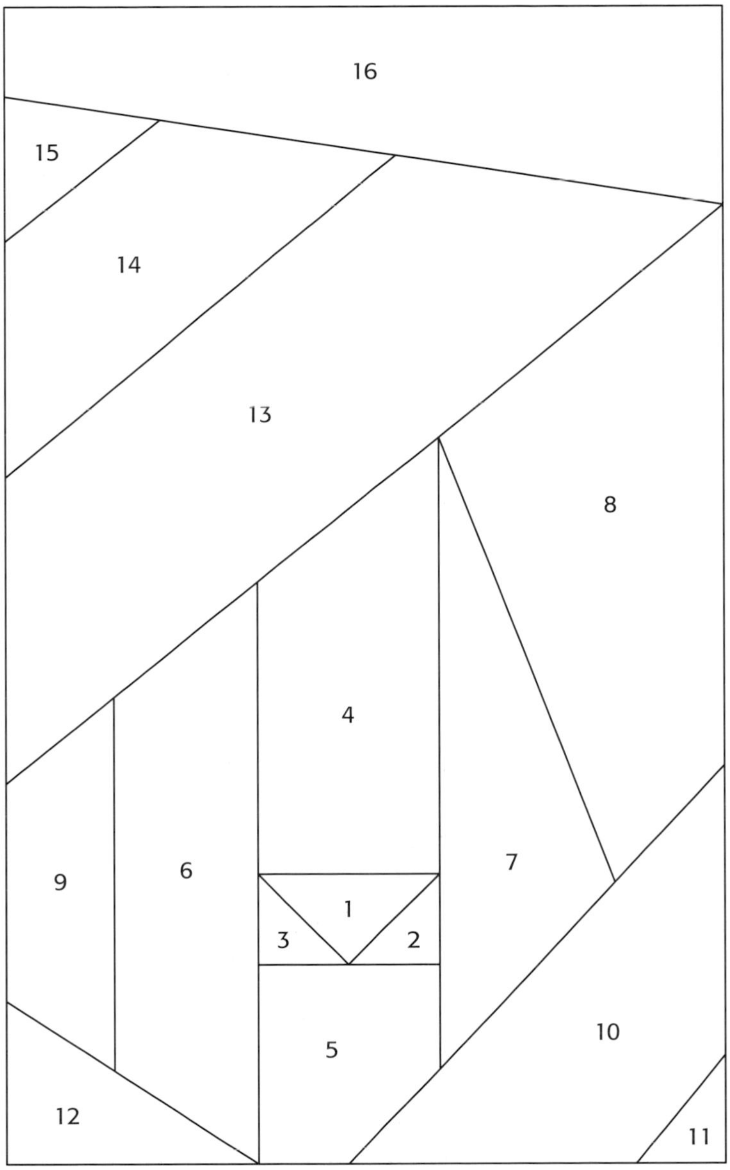

P72A

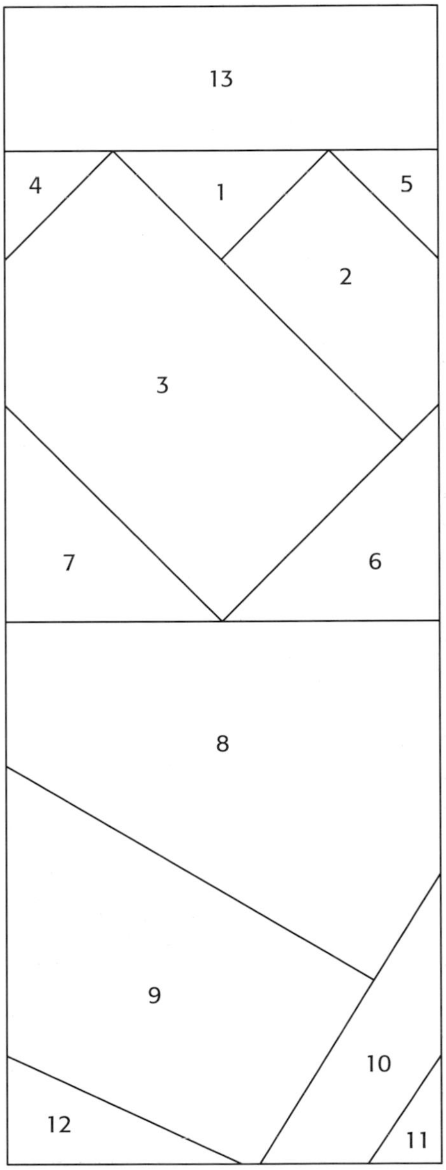

P72B

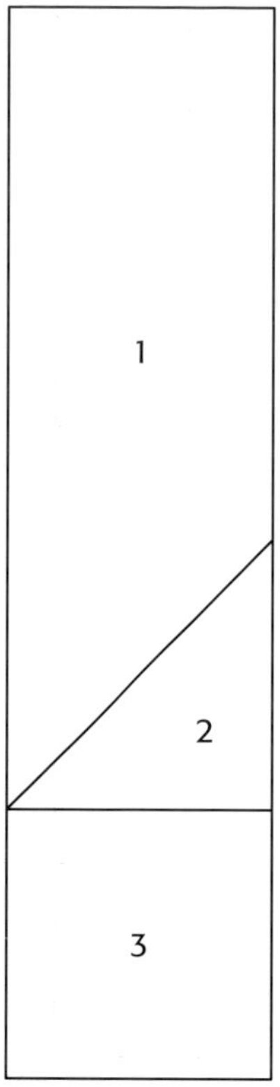

P73A

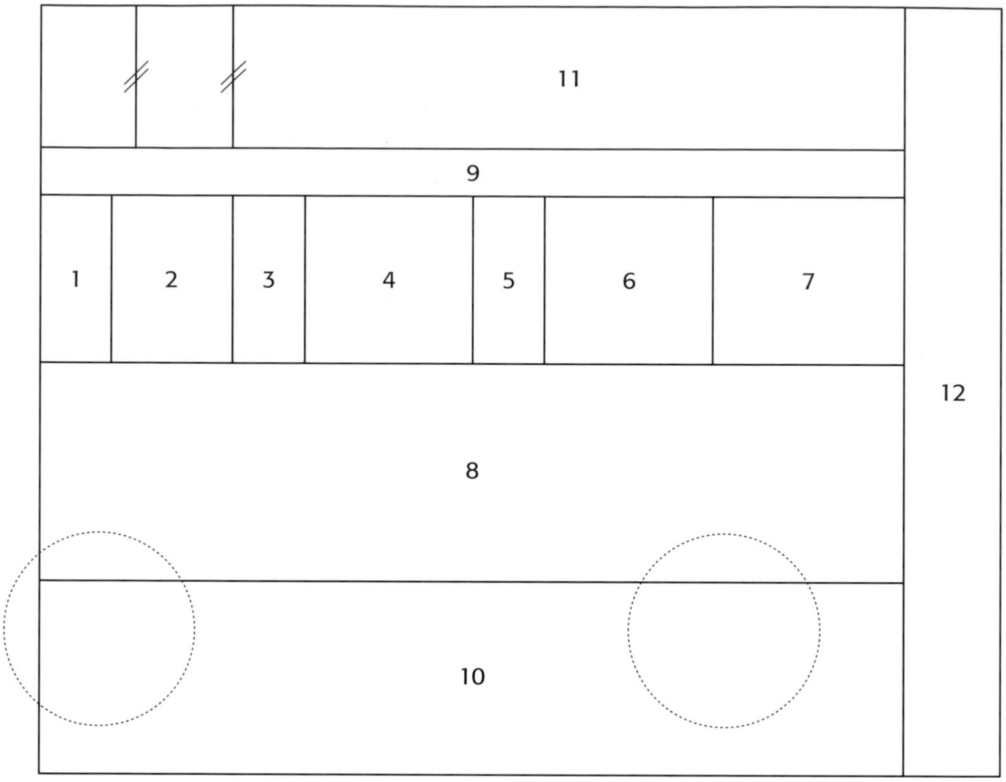

P73B

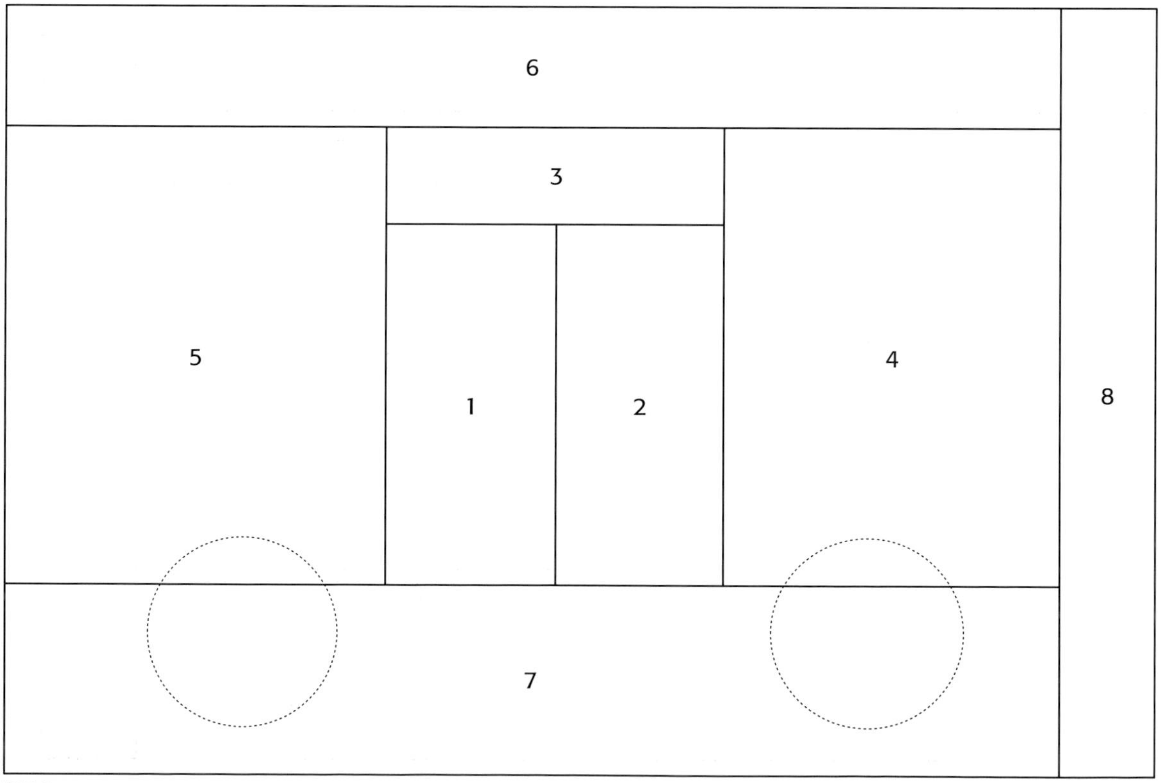

P74

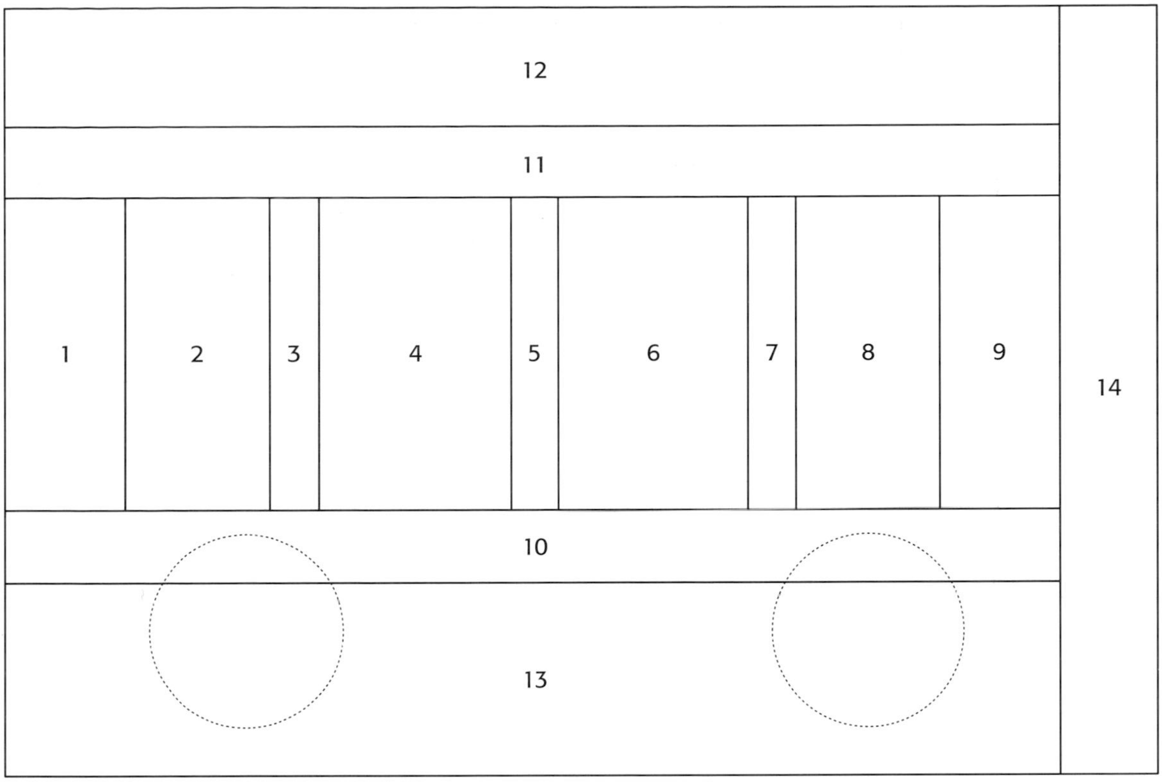

P75

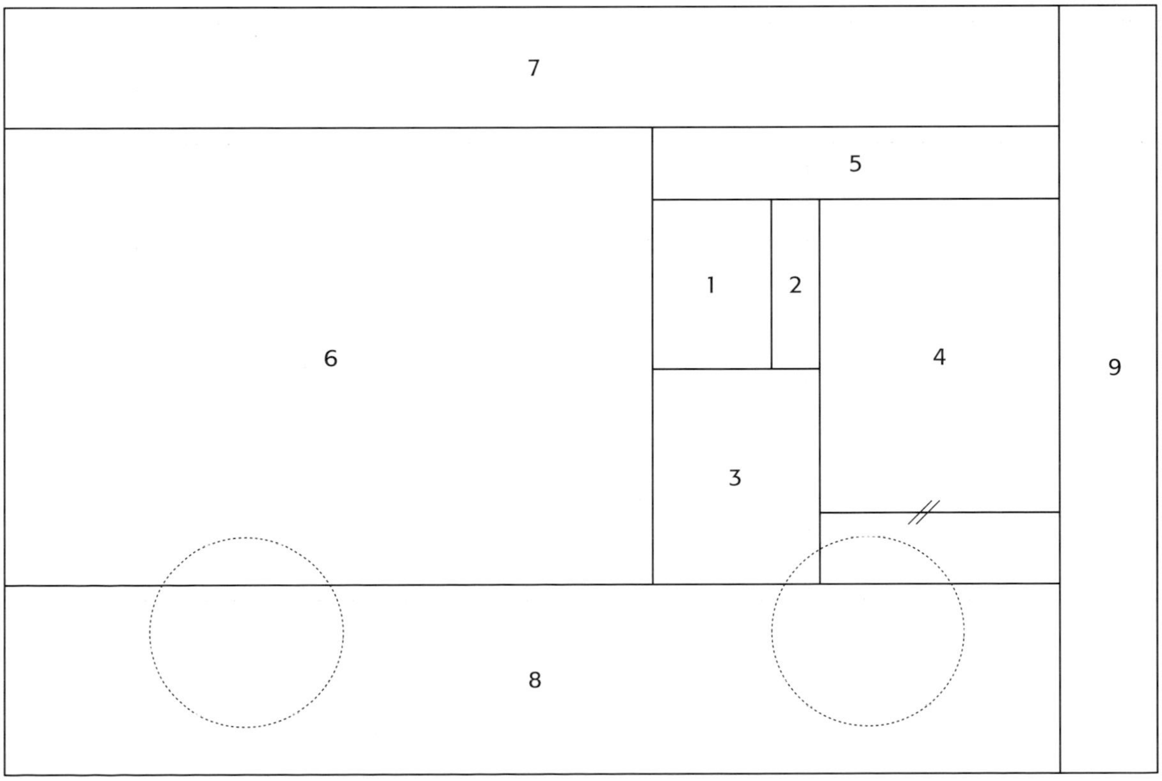

P76

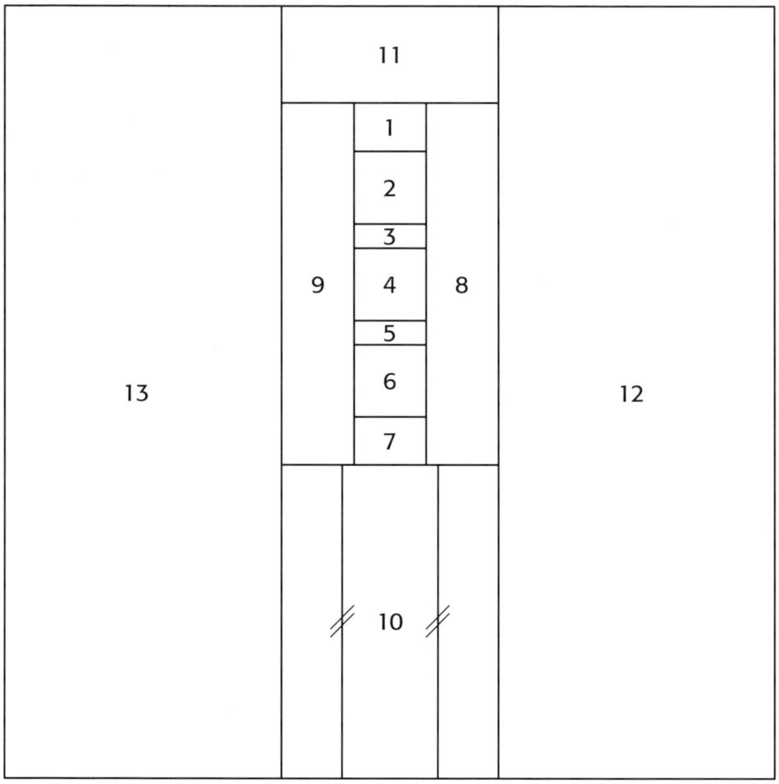

P77

Resources

Carol Doak Designer Edition, Version 3, of the Foundation Factory is available from:

Quilt-Pro Systems, Inc.
P.O. Box 560692
The Colony, TX 75056
Telephone: 800-884-1511
Web site: www.quiltpro.com

System requirements: PC running Windows 95/98/NT4, 8 MB RAM, 25MB available disk space; mouse or other pointing device. High-color or true-color video recommended.

Papers for Foundation Piecing and the 6" Add-a-Quarter™ ruler are available from:
Martingale & Company
20205 144th Avenue NE
Woodinville, WA 98072-8478
800-426-3126

Thread clippers are available from:

Tool Tron Industries
Telephone: 830-249-8277
E-mail: tooltron@texas.net
Web site: www.tooltron.com

Carol Doak's teaching schedule is available on her Web site at the following address:

www.quilt.com/CDoak

MEET THE AUTHOR

Carol with her granddaughter Jessie Ann Doak.

As a bestselling author, celebrated teacher, lecturer, and award-winning quiltmaker, Carol Doak has greatly influenced the art and craft of quiltmaking for more than a decade, both in the U.S. and internationally. Her accomplishments include a sizable collection of popular books: *Easy Machine Paper Piecing, Easy Paper-Pieced Keepsake Quilts, Easy Mix & Match Machine Paper Piecing, Easy Reversible Vests, Show Me How to Paper Piece, Easy Paper-Pieced Miniatures,* and *Your First Quilt Book (or it should be!).* Her most recent books are: *Easy Stash Quilts* and *50 Fabulous Paper-Pieced Stars.* Books in print exceed three-quarters of a million copies! It is no secret that Carol has helped to raise the popularity of paper piecing, her trademark technique, to heights never before seen in the world of quiltmaking.

An impressive range of her beautiful blue-ribbon quilts has been featured in several books and magazines.

If you have ever taken a class from Carol, you know that her enthusiasm for quiltmaking is infectious. Carol has a gift for sharing her inspiring ideas with her students in a positive and unique way.

Carol lives with her husband in Windham, New Hampshire, where the cold winters offer plenty of opportunity to snuggle under a quilt in progress.